Legends of Old Honolulu

Other Mutual Books by
W. D. Westervelt

Legends of Old Honolulu

Collected and Translated from the Hawaiian

W. D. Westervelt

Mutual Publishing

ISBN 1-56647-604-6

Library of Congress Catalog Card
Number: 2003105818

Design by Angela Wu-Ki

First Printing, July 2003
1 2 3 4 5 6 7 8 9

Mutual Publishing
1215 Center Street, Suite 210
Honolulu, Hawaii 96816
Ph: (808) 732-1709
Fax: (808) 734-4094
e-mail: mutual@lava.net
www.mutualpublishing.com

Printed in Australia by McPherson's Printing Group

TABLE OF CONTENTS

FOREWORD
Hawai'i's Sacred Narratives
by Glen Grant

Today's generation has little access to storytellers familiar with Hawai'i's oral narratives. Through these narrators of Hawai'i's past one would learn almost forgotten history of places and events of long ago—that the dramatic peak of Olomana was once a giant thief, slain Goliath-like by a young chief from Kaua'i, that "Chinaman's Hat" (a name that should be forever erased from this historic isle) is the tail of Mokoli'i, a *mo'o* killed by Hi'iaka, the sister of Pele.

These storytellers would provide far more compelling and dramatic understanding of places with present day nomers like "Crouching Lion," "Round Top," "Punchbowl," "Diamond Head," "Yokohama Bay," "Tantalus," "Rainbow Falls" and "Paradise Park." The stories behind these modern place names are neither as interesting nor as insightful as the original Hawaiian ones.

To reconnect with the islands' past in the absence of storytellers perpetuating the oral tradition one goes to the written records of several nineteenth-century collectors of the oral traditions of *mo'olelo* (story, myth) and *ka'ao* (legend, tale). Hawaiian historians, such as David Malo and Samuel M. Kamakau, whose lives bridged both the eighteenth and nineteenth centuries, are the most noted for recording the myths and legends of their people. Published in the Hawaiian-language newspapers of the day, their rich narratives preserved for prosperity the legends of chiefs great and small, the sacred mythologies of gods, and ghost-gods, the infamous battles and rivalries, the folk tales and daily lore of the *maka'ainana* (the people) and how places, stones, beaches and valleys were named. King Kalakaua with his *Myths and Legends of Hawai'i* also added his family traditions to the records of old.

As the Caucasian presence in nineteenth-century Hawai'i radically transformed the islands (leading to the destruction, and disenfranchisement of the native people) several non-Hawaiian scholars recorded the ancient myths and legends for an English-speaking audience. With the then popularity of the Grimm Brothers' first collection of "fairy tales," European and American scholars began to collect the "folklore" of ethnic groups throughout the world. In Hawai'i, the paternalistic belief that the nostalgic remembrance of folk materials would preserve memories of a vanishing people was an added factor.

One of the first foreign scholars of Hawaiian folklore was Abraham Fornander, a former student of a Swedish rectory who abandoned religion for life on a whaling ship. Deserting at Honolulu, in 1844, Fornander settled in the islands, to become a coffee planter, surveyor, newspaper editor, inspector of the schools and a judge. Married to a Hawaiian woman, he was actively involved in native affairs, working with young men such as Malo and Kamakau to collect native lore and history. His *An Account of the Polynesian Race* and *Collection of Hawaiian Antiquities and Folklore*—which is one of the most important and accurate nineteenth century histories—are still vital resources.

Among the more literary renditioners of Hawaiian folklore were Thomas Thrum and William Drake Westervelt, whose works remain the most widely read and reprinted English versions. Westervelt drew upon the collections of Malo, Kamakau, and Fornander to popularize Hawaiian folklore in his *Legends of Maui* (1910). *Legends of Old Honolulu* (1915), *Legends of Gods and Ghost-Gods* (1915), *Hawaiian Legends of Volcanoes* (1916) and *Hawaiian Historical Legends* (1923).

Westervelt obtained his A.B.A. and B.D. degrees at Oberlin College in Oberlin, Ohio, where he was born. Pastor of churches in Cleveland, Ohio and Colorado, he settled in the islands in 1899, marrying a missionary descendant, Caroline D. Castle. As a member of the Hawaiian Board of Missions, he was active in developing a multicultural religious community, serving as superintendent of the Sunday School of the Portuguese Church and giving generously in time and money to Japanese Christian churches, including Makiki Christian Church and the Korean Christian Institute.

Westervelt's interest in Hawaiian lore was an avocation that led to numerous magazine and newspaper articles; many reprinted in his several collections. When he passed away at his Waikiki home in 1939, he was widely eulogized as Hawai'i's foremost authority on island folklore. His anthologies of Hawaiian myths, legends and folk tales represents the very best of the English versions of a Hawaiian view of the sacred and profane. Yet the reader needs to be aware that the tales had been filtered by outsiders who embellished, altered or even censored the original materials. To present the ancient Hawai'i lore to a Victorian or Edwardian audience, it was sometimes necessary to introduce Western Christian notions such as monogamous marriages.

One can only conjecture (not without a smile) the discomfort of these *haole* writers when they presented a Hawaiian tale which in its original version was not confined by moral hypocrisy or pent-up sexuality. Koko Head, for example, was originally called Kohelepelepe ("vagina labia minor") in reference to the time when Pele was attacked by Kamapua'a. To save Pele from being raped by the pig demigod, her older sister Kapo detached her vagina, using it as a decoy to divert Kamapua'a, and then hurled it to O'ahu, where it landed at the current site called Koko Head Crater. The missionary cartographers must have tortured for several days before finally renaming the crater Koko Head.

Recently there has been an effort to translate tales collected in the nineteenth century devoid of the moral sensibilities felt by the earlier *haole* writers. Samuel M. Kamakau's *Stories and Legends of Oahu* includes several "trickster" stories reflective of the more lively and hilarious earthiness of the old Hawaiian storytellers. In one tale, a group of brothers are on a hike in Nu'uanu Valley when the youngest *kolohe* (rascal) brother runs ahead. Later, his older siblings come across a *kukui* tree covered with rich sap. Sampling the gooey substance which the Hawaiians used as gum, they all note that the sap is terribly rancid and spit it out in disgust. When they hear the laughter from the top of the tree, they discover to their dismay that the sap is, in fact, the *kukai* (excrement) of their *kolohe* brother, who has been defecating in the tree! The quick censorship which this tale would have engendered by its *haole* editors and translators is not difficult to imagine. Fortunately the original Hawaiian versions are now becoming more accessible to the non-Hawaiian-language reader.

Whatever their editor's motives, biases or subtle distortions, the stories reprinted in this collection still perpetuate the beauty and mystery of Hawaiian sacred narratives. They serve as an excellent first introduction to the rich treasury of myths, legends, and folk tales which once bonded human life, the islands and the spirit realm into a cosmic unity of purpose.

INTRODUCTION

The ancient Hawaiians were not inventive. They did not study new methods of house-building or farming. They did not seek new tools or new weapons. They could live comfortably as their ancestors lived. But they were imaginative and therefore told many a wonderful tale of gods and goblins and men. Some of these stories were centuries old, and were closely akin to legends told in Tahiti, Samoa, Fiji, New Zealand and many other islands of the Pacific Ocean. Most of them were of course limited to the locality from which they came. The Honolulu legends belong to this class almost entirely, although a student of Polynesian mythology will find many traces of connecting links with the mythology of far distant islands.

The legends of Old Honolulu have been compiled from stories told by the old Hawaiians. Some of them came from those still living, but many have been found in the files of papers published from 1850 to 1870.

The first alphabet for Hawaiians was prepared in 1821. The Hawaiians were taught to read and write their histories and ancient stories as rapidly as possible. This was the result of the labors of the American missionaries. Some of the missionaries, notably Mr. Dibble, sent their pupils out to write down and preserve the old legends and traditions. Between thirty and forty years after the first lesson in the alphabet the Hawaiians were writing articles for papers published regularly in their own language—such as *Ka Hae Hawaii (The Hawaiian Flag), Ke Kuokoa (The Independent), Ka Hoku Pakipika (The Star of the Pacific).* These were followed by many papers down to the present time edited solely by Hawaiians.

Careful research through these papers brings many stories of the past into the hands of students. It is chiefly in this way that these legends of Old Honolulu have been gathered together. This is the result of several years' work of note-taking and compilation.

These legends belong of course to Honolulu people, and will be chiefly interesting to them and those who are acquainted with the city and the island of Oahu. It is hoped that folk-lore lovers the world over will also enjoy comparing these tales with those of other lands.

Sometimes these old stories have been touched up and added to by the Hawaiian story-teller who has had contact with foreign literature, and the reader may trace the influence of modern ideas; but this does not occur frequently.

The legend of "Chief Man-eater" comes the nearest to historic times. Cannibalism was not a custom among the ancient Hawaiians. These are unquestionably sporadic cases handed down in legends.

These legends have been printed in the following papers and magazines: *The Friend, The Paradise of the Pacific, The Mid-Pacific, Thrum's Hawaiian Annual, Historical Society Reports, The Advertiser* and *Star Bulletin*, published in Honolulu.

THE AUTHOR

Chapter 1

THE MIGRATION OF THE HAWAIIANS

The fountain source of the Mississippi has been discovered and rediscovered. The origin of the Polynesian race has been a subject for discovery and rediscovery. The older theory of Malay origin as set forth in the earlier encyclopædias is now recognized as untenable. The Malays followed the Polynesians rather than preceded them. The comparative study of Polynesian legends leads almost irresistibly to the conclusion that the Polynesians were Aryans, coming at least from India to Malasia and possibly coming from Arabia, as Fornander of Hawaii so earnestly argues. It is now accepted that the Polynesians did not originate from Malay parentage, and that they did occupy for an indefinite period the region around the Sunda Straits from Java to the Molucca Islands, and also that the greater portion of the Polynesians was driven out from this region and scattered over the Pacific in the early part of the Christian Era. The legends that cluster around Wakea have greatly aided in making plain some things concerning the disposition of the Polyne-sians. By sifting the legends of Hawaii-loa we learn how the great voyager becomes one of the first Vikings of the Pacific. His home at last is found to be Gilolo of the Molucca Islands. From the legends we become acquainted with Wakea (possibly meaning "noonday," or "the white time") and his wife Papa (earth), the most widely remembered of all the ancestors of the Polynesian race. Their names are found in the legends of the most prominent island groups, and the highest places are granted them among the demi-gods and sometimes among the chief deities. Their deeds belong to the most ancient times— the creation or discovery of the various islands of the Pacific world. Those who worshipped Wakea and Papa are found in such widely separated localities that it must be considered impossible for even a demi-god to have had so many homes. Atea, or Wakea, was one of the highest gods of the Marquesas Islands. Here his name means "light." The Marquesans evidently look back of all their present history and locate Atea in the ancient homeland. Vatea in the Society Islands, Wakea in Hawaii and New Zealand, Makea, Vakea and Akea are phonetic variations of the one name when written down by the students

2

who made a written form for words repeated from generation to generation by word of mouth alone. Even under the name "Wakea" this ancient chief is known in most widely separated islands. The only reasonable explanation for this widespread reference to Wakea is that he was an ancestor belonging in common to all the scattered Polynesians. It seems as if there must have been a period when Wakea was king or chief of a united people. He must have been of great ability and probably was the great king of the United Polynesians. If this were the fact it would naturally result that his memory would be carried wherever the dispersed race might go.

In the myths and legends of the Hervey Islands, Vatea is located near the beginning of their national existence. First of all the Hervey Islanders place Te-ake-ia-roe (The root of all existence). Then there came upon the ancient world Te Vaerua (The breath, or The life). Then came the god time—Te Manawa roa (The long ago). Then their creation legends locate Vari, a woman whose name means "the beginning," a name curiously similar to the Hebrew word "bara," "to create," as in Gen. i. 1. Her children were torn out of her breasts and given homes in the ancient mist-land, with which, without any preparation or introduction, Hawaiki is confused in a part of the legend. It has been suggested that this Hawaiki is

Savaii of the Samoan Islands, from which the
Hervey Islands may have had their origin in a
migration of the Middle Ages. One of the children of Vari dwelt in "a sacred tabu island" and
became the god of the fish. Another sought a
home "where the red parrots' feathers were gathered"—the royal feathers for the high chiefs' garments. Another became the echo-god and lived in
"the hollow gray rocks." Another as the god of the
winds went far out "on the deep ocean." Another,
a girl, found a home, "the silent land," with her
mother. Wakea, or Vatea, the eldest of this family,
remained in Ava-iki (Hawaii), the ancestral
home—"the bright land of Vatea." Here he married Papa. This Ava-iki was to the Her-veyites of
later generations the fiery volcanic under-world.
When the long sea-voyages ceased after some centuries, the islanders realized that Ava-iki was very
closely connected with their history. They had
but a misty idea of far-off lands, and they did
know of earthquakes and lava caves and volcanic
fires—so they located Ava-iki as the secret world
under their islands. This under-world with legendary inconsistency was located on the ocean's
surface, when it became necessary to have their
islands discovered by the descendants of Vatea.
According to the Hervey legends, Vatea was the
father of Lono and Kanaloa, two of the great gods
of the Polynesians. They were twins. Lono had

three sons, whom he sent away. They sailed out through many heavens and from Ava-iki pulled up out of the deep ocean two of the Hervey Islands. The natives of the Hervey group supposed that the horizon around their group enclosed the world. Beyond this world line were heavens and heavens. A daring voyager by sailing through the sky-line would break out from this world into an unknown world or a heaven bounded by new horizons. Strangers "broke through" from heaven, sometimes making use of the path of the sun. Thus about twenty-five generations ago Raa (possibly Laa, the Hawaiian) broke down the horizon's bars and established a line of kings in Raiatea. So also when Captain Cook came to the Hervey Islands the natives said: "Whence comes this strange thing? It has climbed up [come up forcibly] from the thin land, the home of Wakea." He had pierced the western heavens from which their ancestors had come.

When the sons of Lono unexpectedly saw a speck of land far away over the sea, they cried out that here was a place created for them by their deified ancestors. As they came nearer they "pulled up" the islands until they grew to be high mountains rising from the deep waters. In these mountains they found the lava caves and deep chasms which they always said extended down under the seas back to Ava-iki.

They made their caves a passageway for spirits to the fairy home of the dead, and therefore into certain chasms cast the bodies of the dead, that the spirit might more easily find the path to the under-world.

Vatea was a descendant of "the long ago," according to the Hervey legend. Wakea of Hawaii was a son of Kahiko, "the ancient." Wakea's home is more definitely stated in the Hawaiian than in the Hervey legends. He lived in O-Lolo-i-mehani, or The Red Lolo, a name confidently referred by Fornander in "The Polynesian Race" to Gilolo, the principal island of the Moluccas. The Red Lolo, as suggested by Fornander, would refer not alone to volcanic action and its decaying debris, but would fittingly designate the largest and most important island of the group. The fire bursting from many volcanoes in the region of the Sunda Straits was "royal" to the beholders, who felt that divine power was present in the mysterious red flames. Hence all the Polynesian tribes invested the red color with especial dignity as a mark of royalty and pre-eminence. It was on the banners allowed only to chiefs when their boats sailed away to visit distant lands. It was the color of the war cloaks of chiefly warriors. In the recent days of the monarchy of Hawaii, the richest crimson was the only color allowed in upholstering the great throne room. Gilolo might worthily bear the name "The Red Lolo" in Hawaiian story. Here Hawaii-loa, the first of the Polynesian Vikings, had his home. Here the Chieftainess Oupe, a Polynesian princess, dwelt. In O-Lolo Wakea married the grand-daughter of Oupe, whose name was Papa. She is almost as widely known in legends as her husband. Papa was said to be a tabued descendant of Hawaii-loa and therefore superior in rank to Wakea. Papa is described as "very fair and almost white." Her name means "earth," and Wakea's name might mean "noonday." This, with the many experiences through which they both passed, would lay the foundation for a very pretty sun-myth, but we cannot avoid the human aspect of the legends and give them both a more worthy position as ancestors of a scattered people.

Kahiko, the ancient, is recorded as having had three sons, from whom descended the chiefs, the priests and the common people,— the husbandmen,—almost a Shem, Ham and Japheth division. Other legends, however, give Kahiko only two sons, the eldest, Wakea, having power both as chief and priest. All the legends unite in making Wakea the head of the class of chiefs. This would very readily explain the high place held by Wakea throughout Polynesia and also the jealous grasp upon genealogical records maintained by the royal families of the Pacific.

Wakea and Papa are credited with being the creators of many island kingdoms of the Pacific. Sometimes the credit is given partly to a mischievous fisherman-god, Maui, after whom one of the Hawaiian Islands is named. One of the Hawaiian legends goes back to the creation or discovery of Hawaii and ascribes the creation of the world to Wakea and Papa. The two were living together in "Po"—"darkness," or "chaos." Papa brought into existence a gourd calabash including bowl and cover, with the pulp and seeds inside. Wakea threw the cover upward and it became heaven. From the pulp and seeds be made the sky and the sun and moon and stars. From the juice of the pulp he made the rain. The bowl he fashioned into the land and sea. Other legends limit the creative labors of Wakea to the Hawaiian group. With the aid of Papa he established a portion of the islands; then discord entered the royal family and a separation was decided upon. The Hawaiian custom has always been for either chief or chiefess to exercise the right to divorce and to contract the marriage ties. Wakea is said to have divorced Papa by spitting in her face, according to an ancient custom. Wakea selected a chieftainess named Hina, from whom the island

Molokai (the leper island) received the name "Molokai-hina"—the ancient name of the island. Morotai was also an island lying near Gilolo in the Mo-lucca group, and might be the place from which Wakea secured his bride. Papa selected as her new husband a chief named Lua. The ancient name of Oahu (the island upon which Honolulu is located) was "Oahu-a-lua" (The Oahu of Lua). One of the Celebes Islands bears a name for one of its districts very similar to Oahu—"Ouadju." Papa seems to have been partially crazed by her divorce. She marries many husbands. She voyages back and forth between distant islands. In an ancient island, Tahiti, she bears children from whom the Tahitians claim descent. In the Celebes she and her people experience a famine and she is compelled to send to O-Lolo for food. In New Zealand legend she becomes the wife of Langi (Hawaiian Lani, or heaven), a union of "earth" and "heaven." They have six children. Four of these are the chief gods of ancient Hawaii: Kane, "light"; Ku, "the builder"; Lono, "sound"; and Kanaloa. Two of the children are not named in Hawaiian annals, unless it might be that one, Tawhirri, should be represented in Kahili, the tall standard used for centuries as the insignia of very high chief families. The other name, "Haumia," might possibly be Haumea, a second

9

name given to Papa in the legends. The Maoris of New Zealand deify all of these six sons of Lani and Papa.

Ka-ne was "father of forests." He was very strong. In ancient days the sky was not separated from the earth. He lifted up the heavens and pushed down the earth—and thus made space for all things to grow. It was while the sky rested its full weight upon the earth that the leaves started into life, but were flat and thin because there was no chance to become plump and full like the fruit which came later. Here is the foundation for another sun-myth of the Pacific, wherein it might be said light came and separating darkness from the earth brought life into the world. Light could well be "the father of forests." The second son was Tawhirri, "the father of winds and storms." A part of his name was "matea," which might possibly be referred to Wakea. He dwelt in the skies with his father Lani.

The third son was Lono, who was "the father of all cultivated food."

The fourth was Haumia, "the father of uncultivated food"—such food as grew wild in the forests or among the herbs or in the midst of the edible sea-mosses.

The fifth son was Kanaloa, "the father of all reptiles and fishes," at first dwelling in Hawaiki on the land with all his descendants.

The sixth son was Ku "with the red face," "the father of fierce or cruel men." Ku was easily made angry, and after a time waged war against his brothers and their followers. There was great destruction, but Ku could not win the victory alone. He was compelled to call upon Tawhirri, "the father of winds and storms." Fierce men and fierce storms made it difficult for the remainder of the household to escape. The "father of forests" bowed to the earth under the terrific force of hurricanes and tornadoes. The "fathers of foods" buried themselves deep in the ground to escape destruction at the hands of cruel mankind and tempestuous nature. Then came the bitter conflict between the family of Kanaloa and their combined enemies. Cruel men were without pity in the blows dealt against their inferior kindred. At last the fish fled to the sea and sought safety in distant waters, finding homes where the children of Ku did not care to follow. The reptiles fled inland to the secret recesses of the mountains and forests. There they have kept their wild savage life through the centuries even to the present day, as in Sumatra, Borneo, the Celebes, the Philippines and other sections of the region around the Sunda Straits. They are not now ocean lovers any more than in the ages past. They do not "go down to the sea in ships."

11

Neither do they love the coming of Dutch or Spanish or American civilization. They seem to have an hereditary dislike for strange and cruel men.

The sea rovers became great wanderers, carrying with them the name of "Kanaloa" and planting it in almost all the Pacific islands to be worshipped as one of the supreme gods.

How much these domestic troubles surrounding the name of Papa may have had to do with an early migration of the Polynesians we do not know. It may be that while the household was engaged in war the Malays came from the north and with tornado power scattered the divided family, compelling swift flight to distant lands. It is now understood that the great dispersion of the Polynesians came from the incursions of the powerful Malays during the second century of the Christian Era. Some of the Hawaiian and New Zealand legends imply that for a number of generations a part of the Polynesians remained in the old family home, Hawaiki. The New Zealanders enter quite fully into the account of the troubles attending the coming of their ancestors from Hawaiki. They mention battles and domestic discords. They tell of the long journeys and wearisome efforts put forth until their ancestors find Northern New Zealand, Ke-ao-tea-roa (The great white land).

This was pulled up out of the sea for them by Maui with his wonderful fish-hook. This story of the magic fishing of the disobedient and mischievous Maui is common in Polynesia.

After the discovery of New Zealand, boats were sent back to Hawaiki to induce large corn-panics of colonists to leave the land of warfare and trouble and settle in rich lands bordering the beautiful bays of New Zealand.

Like stories of discovery of new lands and return for friends adorn the legends of all Polynesia. Wakea's descendants were clannish and stood by each other in that great migration of the second century as well as in the better-remembered journeys of later years. There seems to have been a continued migration of the Polynesians. Sometimes they were apparently fought off by the black race, as in Australia; sometimes they held their own for a time, keeping the black men inland, as in Fiji; and sometimes they struck out boldly for new lands, as when they sailed long distances to the Hawaiian and Easter Islands. It is said that the purest forms of the Polynesian language, most harmonious with one another, were carried by the children of Wakea to the far distant islands of New Zealand, Hawaii and Easter Island.

Chapter 2

LEGENDARY PLACES IN HONOLULU

Ho-no-lu-lu is a name made by the union of the
two words "Hono" and "lulu." Some say it
means "Sheltered Hollow." The old Hawaiians
say that "Hono" means "abundance" and "lulu"
means "calm," or "peace," or "abundance of
peace." The navigator who gave the definition
"Fair Haven" was out of the way, inasmuch as
the name does not belong to a harbor, but to a
district having "abundant calm," or "a pleasant
slope of restful land."

"Honolulu" was probably a name given to a
very rich district of farm land near what is now
known as the junction of Liliha and School
Streets, because its chief was Honolulu, one of
the high chiefs of the time of Kakuhihewa,
according to the legends. Kamakau, the
Hawaiian historian, describes this farm district
thus: "Honolulu was a small district, a pleasant
land looking toward the west,—a fat land, with
flowing streams and springs of water, abundant

14

water for taro patches. Mists resting inland breathed softly on the flowers of the hala-tree."

Kakuhihewa was a king of Oahu in the long, long ago, and was so noted that for centuries the island Oahu has been named after him "The Oahu of Kakuhihewa." He divided the island among his favorite chiefs and officers, who gave their names to the places received by them from the king. Thus what is now known as Honolulu was until the time of Kamehameha I., about the year 1800, almost always mentioned as Kou, after the chief Kou, who was an ilamuku (marshal), under King Kakuhihewa. Kou appears to have been a small district, or, rather, a chief's group of houses and grounds, loosely defined as lying between Hotel Street and the sea and between Nuuanu Avenue and Alakea Street.

Ke-kai-o-Mamala was the name of the surf which came in the outer entrance of the harbor of Kou. It was named after Mamala, a chiefess who loved to play konane (Hawaiian checkers), drink awa, and ride the surf. Her first husband was the shark-man Ouha, who later became a shark-god, living as a great shark outside the reefs of Waikiki and Koko Head. Her second husband was the chief Hono-kau-pu, to whom the king gave the land east of Kou, which afterward bore the name of its chief. In this section of Kou now called Honolulu were several very interesting places.

15

Kewalo was the place where the Kauwa, a very low class of servants, were drowned by holding their heads under water. The custom was known as "Ke-kai-heehee," "kai" meaning "sea" and "hee" "sliding along," hence the sliding of the servants under the waves of the sea. Kewalo was also the nesting-ground of the owl who was the cause of a battle between the owls and the king Kakuhihewa, where the owls from Kauai to Hawaii gathered together and defeated the forces of the king.

Toward the mountains above Kewalo lies Makiki plain, the place where rats abounded, living in a dense growth of small trees and shrubs. This was a famous place for hunting rats with bows and arrows.

Ula-kua, the place where idols were made, was near the lumber-yards at the foot of the present Richards Street.

Ka-wai-a-hao (The water belonging to Hao), the site of the noted old native church, was the location of a fine fountain of water belonging to a chief named Hao.

Ke-kau-kukui was close to Ula-kua, and was the place where small konane (checker) boards were laid. These were fiat stones with rows of little holes in which a game was played with black and white stones. Here Mamala and Ouha drank awa and played konane, and

16

Kekuanaoa, father of Kamehameha V., built his home.

Kou was probably the most noted place for konane on Oahu. There was a famous stone almost opposite the site of the temple. Here the chiefs gathered for many a game. Property and even lives were freely gambled away. The Spreckels Building covers the site of this well-known gambling resort.

In Hono-kau-pu was one of the noted places for rolling the flat-sided stone disc known as "the maika stone." This was not far from Richards and Queen Streets, although the great "Ulu-maika" place for the gathering of the chiefs was in Kou. This was a hard, smooth track about twelve feet wide extending from the corner of Merchant and Fort Streets now occupied by the Bank of Hawaii along the seaward side of Merchant Street to the place beyond Nuuanu Avenue known as the old iron works at Ula-ko-heo. It was used by the highest chiefs for rolling the stone disc known as "the maika stone." Kamehameha I. is recorded as having used this maika track.

Ka-ua-nono-ula (rain-with-the-red-rainbow) was the place in this district for the wai-lua, or ghosts, to gather for their nightly games and sports. Under the shadows of the trees, near the present Hawaiian Board Mission rooms at the junction of Alakea and Merchant Streets, these ghosts made night a source of dread to all the people. Another place in Honolulu for the gathering of ghosts was at the corner of King Street and Nuuanu Avenue.

Puu-o-wai-na, or Punchbowl, was a "hill of sacrifice" or "offering," according to the meaning of the native words, and not "Wine-hill" as many persons have said. Kamakau, a native historian of nearly fifty years ago, says: "Formerly there was an imu ahi, a fire oven, for burning men on this hill. Chiefs and common people were burned as sacrifices in that noted place. Men were brought for sacrifice from Kauai, Oahu, and Maui, but not from Hawaii. People could be burned in this place for violating the tabus of the tabu divine chiefs."

"The great stone on the top of Punchbowl Hill was the place for burning men."

Part of an ancient chant concerning Punchbowl reads as follows:

> "O the raging tabu fire of Keaka,
>   O the high ascending fire of the sacrifice!
>   Tabu fire, scattered ashes.
>   Tabu fire, spreading heat."

Nuuanu Valley is full of interesting legendary places. The most interesting, however, is the little valley made by a mountain spur pushing its way out from the Kalihi foothills into the larger valley, and bearing the name "Waolani," the wilderness home of the gods, and now the home of Honolulu's Country Club. This region belonged to the eepa people. These were almost the same as the ill-shaped, deformed or injured gnomes of European fairy tales. In this beautiful little valley which opened into Nuuanu Valley was the heiau Waolani built for Ka-hanai-a-ke-Akua (The chief brought up by the gods), long before the days of Kakuhihewa. It was said that the two divine caretakers of this chief were Kahano and Newa, and that Kahano was the god who lay down on the ocean, stretching out his hands until one rested on Kahiki (Tahiti or some other foreign land) and the other rested on Oahu. Over his arms as a great bridge walked the Menehunes, or fairy people, to Oahu. They came to be servants for this young chief who was in the care of the gods. They built fish-ponds and temples. They lived in Manoa Valley and on Punchbowl Hill. Ku-leo-nui (Ku-with-the-loud-voice) was their master. He could call them any evening. His voice was heard over all the island. They came at once and almost invariably finished each task before the rays of the rising sun drove them to their hidden resorts in forest or wilderness.

Waolani heiau was the place where the noted legendary musical shell "Kiha-pu" had its first home—from which it was stolen by Kapuni and carried to its historic home in Waipio Valley, Hawaii. Below Waolani Heights, the Menehunes built the temple Ka-he-iki for the "child-nourished-by-the-gods," and here the priest and prophet lived who founded the priest-clan called "Mo-o-kahuna," one of the most sacred clans of the ancient Hawaiians. Not far from this temple was the scene of the dramatic plea of an owl for her eggs when taken from Kewalo by a man who had found her nest. It forms part of the story of the battle of the owls and the king.

Nearer the banks of the Nuuanu stream was the great bread-fruit tree into which a woman thrust her husband by magic power when he was about to be slain and offered as sacrifice to the gods. This tree became one of the most powerful wooden gods of the Hawaiians, being preserved, it is said, even to the times of Kamehameha I.

At the foot of Nuuanu Valley is Pu-iwa, a place by the side of the Nuuanu stream. Here a father, Maikoha, told his daughters to bury his body, that from it might spring the wauke-*
tree, used for making kapa ever since. From this place, the legend says, the wauke-tree spread over all the islands.

* Mulberry, Broussonetia papyrifera.

In the bed of the Nuuanu is the legendary stone called "The Canoe of the Dragon." This lies among the boulders in the stream not far from the old Kaumakapili Church premises.

In Nuuanu Valley was the fierce conflict between Kawelo, the strong man from Kauai, assisted by two friends, and a band of robbers. In this battle torn-up trees figured as mighty war-clubs.

These are legendary places which border Kou, the ancient Honolulu. Besides these are many more spots of great interest, as in Waikiki and Manoa Valley, but these lie beyond the boundaries of Kou and ancient Honolulu. In Kou itself was the noted Pakaka Temple. This temple was standing on the western side of the foot of Fort Street long after the fort was built from which the street was named. It was just below the fort. Pakaka was owned by Kinau, the mother of Kamehameha V. It was a heiau, or temple, built before the time of Kakuhihewa. In this temple, the school of the priests of Oahu had its headquarters for centuries. The walls of the temple were adorned with heads of men offered in sacrifice.

Enormous quantities of stone were used in the construction of all these heiaus often passed by hand from quarries at great distances so the work of erection was one consuming much time and energy.

According to the latest investigations there were one hundred and eight heiaus on the island of Oahu, some evidences of which may still be traced, showing the far-reaching influence of kings and priests over these primitive people.

Chapter 3

THE GOD OF PAKAKA TEMPLE

Pakaka* was a heiau, or temple. There are several legends connected with this heiau. One of the most interesting is that which tells how the god of the temple came into being.

The story of the god of this temple is a story of voyages and vicissitudes. Olopana had sailed away from Waipio, Hawaii, for the islands of distant seas. Somewhere in all that great number of islands which were grouped under the general name "Kahiki" Olopana found a home. Here his daughter Mu-lei-ula (Mu-with-the-red-garland) was experiencing great trouble being near to childbirth. For some reason Haumea, one of the divine Polynesian ancestors, had stopped for a time to visit the people of that land. When the friends were afraid that Mu-lei-ula would die, Haumea came to help, saying: "In our land the mother lives. The mother and child both live." The people said,

* Foot of Fort Street near lumber yards.

"If you give us aid, how can we render payment or give you a reward?"

Haumea said: "There is a beautiful tree with two strange but glorious flowers, which I like very much. It is 'the tree of changing leaves' with two flowers, one kind singing sharply, and the other singing from time to time. For this tree I will save the life of the chief's daughter and her child."

Gladly the sick girl and her friends promised to give this beautiful tree to Haumea. It was a tree dearly loved by the princess.

Haumea commenced the prayers and incantations which accompanied her treatment of the sick, and the chiefess rapidly grew stronger. This had come so quickly and easily that she repented the gift of the tree with the beautiful flowers, and cried out, "I will not give the tree."

Immediately she began to lose strength, and called to Haumea that she would give the tree if she could be forgiven and healed. However, as strength came to her once more she again felt sorry for her tree and refused to let it go. Again the incantations were broken off and the divine aid withdrawn.

Olopana in agony cried to his daughter: "Give up your tree. Of what use will it be with its flowers if you die?" Then Haumea, with the most powerful incantations, gave her the final strength, and mother and child both lived and became well and strong.

Haumea took the tree and travelled over the far seas to distant Hawaii. On that larger island she found no place to plant the tree. She crossed over to the island Maui, and came to the "four rivers." There she found the awa of the gods and prepared it for drinking, but needed fresh water to mix with it.

She laid her tree on the ground at Puu-kume by the Wai-hee stream and went down after water. When she returned the tree had rooted. While she looked it began to stand up and send forth branches. She built a stone wall around it, to protect it from the winds. When it blossomed Haumea returned to her divine home in Nuumealani,* the land of mists and shadows where the gods dwelt.

By and by a man took his stone axe and went out to cut a tree, perhaps to make a god. He saw a new tree, short and beautiful, and after hours of labor cut it down. The night was coming on, so he left it as it fell and went home.

That night a fierce and mighty storm came down from the mountains. Blood-red were the streams of water pouring down into the valleys. During twenty nights and twenty days the angry rain punished the land above and around Waihee.

* See "Home of the Ancestors," Part II., in Legends of Ghosts and Ghost-Gods.

The river was more than a rushing torrent. It built up hills and dug ravines. It hurled its mighty waves against the wall inside which the tree stood. It crushed the wall, scattered the stones, and bore the tree down one of the deep ravines. The branches were broken off and carried with the trunk of the tree far out into the ocean.

For six months the waves tossed this burden from one place to another, and at last threw the largest branch on the reef near the beach of Kailua, on the island Hawaii. The people saw a very wonderful thing. Where this branch lay stranded in the water, fish of many kinds gathered leaping around it. The chiefs took this wonderful branch inland and made the god Makalei, which was a god of Hawaii for generations.

Another branch came into the possession of some of the Maui chiefs, and was used as a stick for hanging bundles upon. It became a god for the chiefs of Maui, with the name Ku-ke-olo-ewa.

The body of the tree rolled back and forth along the beach near the four waters, and was wrapped in the refuse of the sea.

A chief and his wife had not yet found a god for their home. In a dream they were told to get a god. For three days they consulted priests, repeated prayers and incantations, and offered sacrifices to the great gods, while they made search for wood from which to cut out their god.

On the third night the omens led them down to the beach and they saw this trunk of a tree rolling back and forth. A dim haze was playing over it in the moonlight. They took that tree, cut out their god, and called it Ku-hoo-nee-nuu. They built a heiau, or temple, for this god, and named that heiau Waihau and made it tabu, or a sacred place to which the priests and high chiefs alone were admitted freely.

The mana, or divine power, of this god was very great, and it was a noted god from Hawaii to Kauai. Favor and prosperity rested upon this chief who had found the tree, made it a god, and built a temple for it.

The king who was living on the island Oahu heard about this tree, and sent servants to the island Maui to find out whether or no the reports were true. If true they should bring that god to Oahu.

They found the god and told the chief that the king wanted to establish it at Kou,* and would build a temple for it there. The chief readily gave up his god and it was carried over to its new home.

So the temple, or heiau, was built at Kou and the god Ku-hoo-nee-nuu placed in it. This temple was Pakaka, the most noted temple on the island Oahu, while its god, the log of the tree from a foreign land, became the god of the chiefs of Oahu.

* Ancient Honolulu.

27

Chapter 4

LEGEND OF THE BREAD-FRUIT TREE

The wonderful bread-fruit* tree was a great tree growing on the eastern bank of the rippling brook Puehuehu.† It was a tabu tree, set apart for the high chief from Kou and the chiefs from Honolulu to rest under while on their way to bathe in the celebrated diving-pool Wai-kaha-lulu. That tree became a god, and this is the story of its transformation:

Papa and Wakea were the ancestors of the great scattered sea-going and sea-loving people living in all the islands now known as Polynesia. They had their home in every group of islands where their descendants could find room to multiply.

They came to the island of Oahu, and, according to almost all the legends, were the first residents. The story of the magic bread-fruit tree, however, says that Papa sailed from Kahiki (a far-off land) with her husband Wakea, landing

* Ulu—Artocarpus incisa.   † Near Nuuanu Street Bridge.

28

on Oahu and finding a home in the mountain upland near the precipice Kilohana.

Papa was a kupua—a woman having many wonderful and miraculous powers. She had also several names. Sometimes she was called Hau-mea, but at last she left her power and a new name, Ka-meha-i-kana, in the magic bread-fruit tree.

Papa was a beautiful woman, whose skin shone like polished dark ivory through the flowers and vines and leaves which were the only clothes she knew. Where she and her husband had settled down they found a fruitful country—with bananas and sugar-cane and taro.* They built a house on the mountain ridge and feasted on the abundance of food around them. Here they rested well protected when rains were falling or the hot sun was shining.

Papa day by day looked over the seacoast which stretches away in miles of marvellous beauty below the precipices of the northern mountain range of the island Oahu. Clear, deep pools, well filled with most delicate fish, lay restfully among moss-covered projections of the bordering coral reef. The restless murmur of surf waves beating in and out through the broken lines of the reef called to her, so,

* Colocasia antiquorum.

29

catching up some long leaves of the hala-tree, she made a light basket and hurried down to the sea. In a little while she had gathered sea-moss and caught all the crabs she wished to take home.

She turned toward the mountain range and carried her burden to Hoakola, where there was a spring of beautiful dear, cold, fresh water. She laid down her moss and crabs to wash them clean.

She looked up, and on the mountain-side discerned there something strange. She saw her husband in the hands of men who had captured and bound him and were compelling him to walk down the opposite side of the range. Her heart leaped with fear and anguish. She forgot her crabs and moss and ran up the steep way to her home. The moss rooted itself by the spring, but the crabs escaped to the sea.

On the Honolulu side of the mountains were many chiefs and their people, living among whom was Lele-hoo-mao, the ruler, whose fields were often despoiled by Papa and her husband. It was his servants who while searching the country around these fields, had found and captured Wakea. They were forcing him to the temple Pakaka* to be there offered in sacrifice.

* The Pakaka temple through its hundreds of years of existence received from time to time human sacrifice.

They were shouting, "We have found the mischiefmaker and have tied him."

Papa threw around her some of the vines which she had fashioned into a skirt, and ran over the hills to the edge of Nuuanu Valley.

Peering down the valley she saw her husband and his captors, and cautiously she descended.

She found a man by the side of the stream Puehuehu, who said to her: "A man has been carried by who is to be baked in an oven this day. The fire is burning in the valley below."

Papa said, "Give me water to drink."

The man said, "I have none."

Then Papa took a stone and smashed it against the ground. It broke through into a pool of water. She drank and hastened on to the breadfruit tree at Nini, where she overtook her husband and the men who guarded him. He was alive, his hands bound behind him and his leaf clothing torn from his body. Wailing and crying that she must kiss him, she rushed to him and began pushing and pulling him, whirling him around and around.

Suddenly the great bread-fruit tree opened and she leaped with him through the doorway into the heart of the tree. The opening closed in a moment.

Papa, by her miraculous power, opened the tree on the other side. They passed through and went rapidly up the mountain-side to their home, which was near the head of Kalihi Valley.

As they ran Papa threw off her vine pa-u, or skirt. The vine became the beautiful morning-glory, delicate in blossom and powerful in medicinal qualities. The astonished men had lost their captive. According to the ancient Hawaiian proverb, "Their fence was around the field of nothingness." They pushed against the tree, but the opening was tightly closed. They ran around under the heavy-leaved branches and found nothing. They believed that the great tree held their captive in its magic power.

Quickly ran the messenger to their high chief, Lele-hoo-mao, to tell him about the trouble at the tabu bread-fruit tree at Nini and that the sacrifice for which the oven was being heated was lost.

The chiefs consulted together and decided to cut down that tree and take the captive out of his hiding-place. They sent tree-cutters with their stone axes.

The leader of the tree-cutters struck the tree with his stone axe. A chip leaped from the tree, struck him, and he fell dead.

Another caught the axe. Again chips flew and the workman fell dead.

Then all the cutters struck and gashed the tree.

Whenever a chip hit any one he died, and the sap of the tree flowed out and was spattered under the blows of the stone axes. Whenever a drop touched a workman or a bystander he fell dead.

The people were filled with fear and cried to their priest for help.

Wohi, the priest, came to the tree, bowed before it, and remained in silent thought a long time. Then he raised his head and said: "It was not a woman who went into that tree. It was Papa from Kahiki. She is a goddess and has a multitude of bodies. If we treat her well we shall not be destroyed."

Wolff commanded the people to offer sacrifices at the foot of the tree. This was done with prayers and incantations. A black pig, black awa and red fish were offered to Papa. Then Wolff commanded the wood-cutters to rub themselves bountifully with coconut oil and go fearlessly to their work. Chips struck them and the sap of the tree was spattered over them, but they toiled on unhurt until the great tree fell.

Out of this magic bread-fruit tree a great goddess was made. Papa gave to it one of her names, Ka-meha-i-kana, and endowed it with power so that it was noted from Kauai to Hawaii. It became one of the great gods of Oahu, but was taken to Maui, where Kamehameha secured it as his god to aid in establishing his rule over all the islands.

The peculiar divine gift supposed to reside in this image made from the wonderful breadfruit tree was the ability to aid worshippers in winning land and power from other people and wisely employing the best means of firmly establishing their own government, thus protecting and preserving the kingdom.

Papa dwelt above the Kalihi Valley and looked down over the plains of Honolulu and Ewa covered with well-watered growing plants which gave food or shade to the multiplying people.

It is said that after a time she had a daughter, Kapo, who also had kupua, or magic power. Kapo had many names, such as Kapo-ula-kinau and Laka. She was a high tabu goddess of the ancient Hawaiian hulas, or dances. She had also the power of assuming many bodies at will and could appear in any form from the mo-o, or lizard, to a human being.

Note: Kapo is the name of a place and of a wonderful stone with a "front like the front of a house and a back like the tail of a fish." The legends of sixty years ago say that Kapo still stood in that place as one of the guardians of Kalihi Valley.

Kapo was born from the eyes of Haumea, or Papa.

Papa looked away from Kapo and there was born from her head a sharp pali, or precipice, often mist-covered; this was Ka-moho-alii. Then Pele was born. She was the one who had mighty battles with Kamapuaa, the pig-man, who almost destroyed the volcano Kilauea. It was Ka-moho-alii who rubbed sticks and rekindled the volcanic fires for his sister Pele, thus driving Kamapuaa down the sides of Kilauea into the ocean.

These three, according to the Honolulu legends, were the highest-born children of Papa and Wakea.

Down the Kalihi stream below Papa's home were two stones to which the Hawaiians gave eepa, or gnomelike, power. If any traveller passes these stones on his way up to Papa's resting-place, that wayfarer stops by these stones, gathers leaves and makes leis, or garlands, and places them on these stones, that there may be no trouble in all that day's wanderings.

Sometimes mischievous people dip branches from lehua-trees in water and sprinkle the eepa rocks; then woe to the traveller, for piercing rains are supposed to fall. From this comes the proverb belonging to the residents of Kalihi Valley, "Here is the sharp-headed rain of Kalihi" ("Ka ua poo lipilipi o Kalihi").

Chapter 5

THE GODS WHO FOUND WATER

Four great gods with a large retinue of lesser gods came from Kahiki to the Hawaiian Islands. "Kahiki" meant any land beyond the skies which came down to the seas around the Hawaiian group. These gods settled for a time in Nuuanu Valley, back of the lands now known as Honolulu. These four great gods were worshipped by the Polynesians scattered all over the Pacific Ocean. Their names were Ku, Lono, Ka-ne and Kanaloa.

Kaone and Kanaloa were the water-finders, opening springs and pools over all the islands, each pool known now as Ka-Wai-a-ke-Akua (The water provided by a god).

In one of the very old Hawaiian newspapers the question was asked, "What are the waters of Ka-ne?" The answers came: The heavy showers of life-giving rain, the mountain stream swelling into a torrent lifting and carrying away canoes, the rainbow-colored rain loved by Ka-ne, the continually flowing brooks of the valleys and the fresh waters found anywhere—these were the waters of Ka-ne.

It may reasonably be surmised that from the realization of the blessing of fresh waters the ancient Polynesians as well as the Hawaiians looked up to some waters to be found somewhere in the lands of the gods, which were called "the waters of life of Ka-ne." The Hawaiian legends said: "If any one is dead and this water is thrown upon him, he becomes alive again. Old people bathing in this water go back to their youth." If the common fresh water of the hills and plains was good, it was easy to look beyond to something better.

The gods Ka-ne and Kanaloa were very closely allied to the farming interests of the people of the long ago. Prayers were offered to them in all the different stages of the process of farming. When a field was selected some article of food was cooked and offered with the prayer:

"Here is food,
  O Gods, Ka-ne and Kanaloa!
  Here is food for us.
  Give life to us and our family.
  Life for the parents feeble with age.
  Life for all in the household.
  When digging and planting our land
  Life for us—
  This is our prayer. Amama."

A similar prayer was made while cultivating the crops or harvesting the ripened product.

It may be that the close connection of waters with plant growth made these two gods the especial gods of farmers.

There was a host of other gods whose names were sometimes used in prayers offered while farming. Each of these gods bore the name "Kane" (sometimes Ku or Lono would be substituted), followed by an adjective showing some method of work, but all these names of lesser gods were apparently used to explain the particular task desired, as when the name "Ka-ne-apuaa" was mentioned in some prayers, the word "puaa" (pig) carried the idea of digging or uprooting the soil.

Ka-ne and Kanaloa were great travellers. Together they journeyed over Kauai, coming (according to an account written in the Kuokoa about 1868 by the Rev. J. Waiamau) from faraway lands. They appeared more like men than gods, and the Kauai people did not worship them, so they opened up only a few springs and crossed over to the island Oahu.

Throughout all the islands the awa root has been found. It was bitter and very astringent, but when crushed and mixed with water the juice became a liquor greatly loved by the people. "These two gods drank awa from Kauai to Hawaii," so the old legends say.

They journeyed along the coast of the island Oahu until they came to Kalihi, one of the present suburbs of the city of Honolulu. For a long time they had been looking up the hillsides and along the water courses for awa*—but had not found what seemed desirable.

At Kalihi a number of fine awa roots were growing. They pulled up the roots and prepared them for chewing. When the awa was ready Kanaloa looked for fresh water, but could not find any. So he said to Ka-ne: "Our awa is good, but there is no water in this place. Where can we find water for this awa?"

Ka-ne said, "There is indeed water here." He had a "large and strong staff," in some of the legends called a spear. This he took in his hands and stepped out on the bed of lava which now underlies the soil of that region. He began to strike the earth. Deep went the point of his staff into the rock, smashing and splintering it and breaking open a hole out of which water leaped for them to mix with their prepared awa. This pool of fresh water has been known since the days of old as Ka - puka - Wai - o - Kalihi (The water door of Kalihi). The gods, stupefied by the liquor, lay down and slept. When at last they were weary of that resting-place, they passed Nuuanu Valley and went into the most beautiful

* Piper Methysticum.

rainbow valley of the world, Manoa Valley, the home of the rainbow princess. This valley is one of the well-settled suburbs of Honolulu.

Well-wooded precipices guard the upper end of the valley and make difficult the path to the tops of the mountains rising thousands of feet above.

Here the gods found most excellent awa, and Kanaloa cried, "O my brother, this is awa surpassing any other we have found; but where shall I go to find water?" Ka-ne replied, "Here in this hillside is water." So he took his "staff and struck it fiercely against the precipice by which they had found awa. Rapidly the rocks were broken off. The precipice crept back from the mighty strokes of the god and a large pool of dear, cool water appeared among the great stones which had fallen. There they mixed awa and water and drank again and again until the sleep of the drunkard came and they rested by the fountain they had made. This pool is still at the head of Manoa Valley, and to this day is called Ka-Wai-a-ke-Akua (The water provided by a god).

The servants of hundreds of chiefs have borne water from this place to their thirsty masters.

In the days of Kamehameha I. very often messengers came from this pool of water of the gods with calabashes full of water swinging from the ends of sticks laid over their shoulders.

When they came near any individual or group of Hawaiians they had to call out loudly, giving warning so that all by whom they passed could fall prostrate before the gift of the gods to the great king.

Ka-ne and Kanaloa made many springs of fresh waters in all the different islands. Sometimes a watchman refused to let them take the desired awa—the legends say that they called such persons stingy, and caught them and put them to death. At Honuaula they broke a large place and made a great fish-pond.

They went to Kohala, Hawaii, and found a temple in which they lived for a long time, and the people of Hawaii thought they were gods. Therefore they brought sacrifices and offered worship, and Ka-ne and Kanaloa were satisfied to remain as two of the gods of the islands.

This idea of "striking a rock for water springs" is not connected with or derived in any way from Biblical sources. The tool used by Hawaiians for centuries for digging was called the o-o which was but little more than a sharp-pointed stick or staff, which was a lever as well as a spade. There is nothing in the legend beyond the expression of a desire to locate water springs as a gift from the gods.

Chapter 6

THE WATER OF LIFE OF KA-NE

A Legend of Old Hawaii

"When the moon dies she goes to the living water of Ka-ne, to the water which can restore all to life, even the moon to the path in the sky."—*Maori Legend of New Zealand.*

The Hawaiians of long ago shared in the belief that somewhere along the deep sea beyond the horizon around their islands, or somewhere in the cloud-land above the heavens which rested on their mountains, there was a land known as "The land of the water of life of the gods." In this land was a lake of living water in which always rested the power of restoration to life. This water was called in the Hawaiian language Ka wai ola a Ka-ne, literally "The water living of Ka-ne," or "The water of life of Ka-ne."

Mention of this "wai ola" is found in many of the Pacific island groups, such as New Zealand, the Tongas, Samoa, Tahiti and the Hawaiian Islands. The thought of "water of life" cannot be limited to only a few references in legends.

43

Some of the most interesting legendary experiences in several island groups belong to the stories of a search after this "water of life."

Ka-ne was one of the four greatest gods of the Polynesians. In his hands was placed the care of the water of life. If any person secured this water, the power of the god went with it. A sick person drinking it would recover health, and a dead person sprinkled with it would be restored to life.

In the misty past of the Hawaiian Islands a king was very, very ill. All his friends thought that he was going to die. The family came together in the enclosure around the house where the sick man lay. Three sons were wailing sorely because of their heavy grief.

An old man, a stranger, passing by asked them the cause of the trouble. One of the young men replied, "Our father lies in that house very near death."

The old man looked over the wall upon the young men and said slowly: "I have heard of something which would make your father well. He must drink of the water of life of Ka-ne. But this is very hard to find and difficult to get."

The old man disappeared, but the eldest son said, "I shall not fail to find this water of life, and I shall be my father's favorite and shall have the kingdom." He ran to his father for permission to go and find this water of life.

The old king said: "No, there are many difficulties and even death in the way. It is better to die here." The young prince urged his father to let him try, and at last received permission.

The prince, taking his water calabash, hastened away. As he went along a path through the forest, suddenly an ugly little man, a dwarf (an a-a), appeared in his path and called out, "Where are you going that you are in such a hurry?" The prince answered roughly: "Is this your business? I have nothing to say to you." He pushed the little man aside and ran on.

The dwarf was very angry and determined to punish the rough speaker, so he made the path twist and turn and grow narrow before the traveller. The further the prince ran, the more bewildered he was, and the more narrow became the way, and thicker and thicker were the trees and vines and ferns through which the path wound. At last he fell to the earth, crawling and fighting against the tangled masses of ferns and the clinging tendrils of the vines of the land of fairies and gnomes. They twined themselves around him and tied him tight with living coils, and finally he lay like one who was dead.

For a long time the family waited and at last came to the conclusion that he had been overcome by some difficulty. The second son said that he would go and find that water of life, so taking his water calabash he ran swiftly along the path which his brother had taken. His thought was also the selfish one, that he might succeed where his brother had failed and so win the kingdom.

As he ran along he met the same little man, who was the king of the fairies although he appeared as a dwarf. The little man called out, "Where are you going in such a hurry?"

The prince spoke roughly, pushed him out of the way, and rushed on. Soon he also was caught in the tangled woods and held fast like one who was dead.

Then the last, the youngest son, took his calabash and went away thinking that he might be able to rescue his brothers as well as get the water of life for his father. He met the same little man, who asked him where he was going. He told the dwarf about the king's illness and the report of the "water of life of Ka-ne," and asked the dwarf if he could aid in any way. "For," said the prince, "my father is near death, and this living water will heal him and I do not know the way."

The little man said: "Because you have spoken gently and have asked my help and have not been rough and rude as were your brothers, I will tell you where to go and will give you aid. The path will open before you at the bidding of this strong staff which I give you. By and by you

will come to the palace of a king who is a sorcerer. In his house is the fountain of that water
of life. You cannot get into that house unless
you take three bundles of food which I will give
you. Take the food in one hand and your strong
staff in the other. Strike the door of that king's
house three times with your staff and an opening will be made. Then you will see two dragons
with open mouths ready to devour you. Quickly
throw food in their mouths and they will
become quiet. Fill your calabash with the living
water and hurry away. At midnight the doors
will be shut, and you cannot escape."

The prince thanked the little man, took the
presents and went his way rejoicing, and after a
long time he came to the strange land and the
sorcerer's house. Three times he struck until he
broke the wall and made a door for himself. He
saw the dragons and threw the food into their
mouths, making them his friends. He went in
and saw some young chiefs, who welcomed him
and gave him a war-club and a bundle of food.
He went on to another room, where he met a
beautiful maiden whom he loved at once with
all his heart. She told him as she looked in his
eyes that after a time they would meet again and
live as husband and wife. Then she showed him
where he could get the water of life, and warned
him to be in haste. He dipped his calabash in

the spring and leaped through the door just at the stroke of midnight.

With great joy he hastened from land to land and from sea to sea watching for the little man, the a-a, who had aided him so much. As if his wish were known soon the little man appeared and asked him how he fared on his journey. The prince told him about the long way and his success and then offered to pay as best he could for all the aid so kindly given.

The dwarf refused all reward. Then the prince said he would be so bold as to ask one favor more. The little man said, "You have been so thoughtful in dealing with me as one highly honored by you, ask and perhaps I can give you what you wish."

The prince said, "I do not want to return home without my brothers; can you help me find them?" "They are dead in the forest," said the dwarf. "If you find them they will only do you harm. Let them rest in their beds of vines and ferns. They have evil hearts."

But the young chief pressed his kindly thought and the dwarf showed him the tangled path through the forest. With his magic staff he opened the way and found his brothers. He sprinkled a little of the water of life over them and strength returned to them. He told them how he had found the "living water of Ka-ne," and had received gifts and also the promise of a beautiful bride. The brothers forgot their long death-like sleep and were jealous and angry at the success of their younger brother.

They journeyed far before they reached home. They passed a strange land where the high chief was resisting a large body of rebels. The land was lying desolate and the people were starving. The young prince pitied the high chief and his people and gave them a part of the bundle of food from the house of the god Ka-ne. They ate and became very strong. Then he let the chief have his war-club. Quickly the rebels were destroyed and the land had quiet and peace.

He aided another chief in his wars, and still another in his difficulties, and at last came with his brothers to the seacoast of his own land. There they lay down to sleep, but the wicked brothers felt that there were no more troubles in which they would need the magic aid of their brother, so they first planned to kill him, but the magic war-club seemed to defend him. Then they took his calabash of the water of life and poured the water into their water-jars, filling his calabash again with salt, sickish sea-water. They went on home the next morning. The young prince pressed forward with his calabash, gave it to his father, telling him to drink and recover life. The king drank deeply of the salt water and was made more seriously sick, almost to death. Then the older brothers came, charging the young prince with an attempt to poison his father. They gave him the real water of life and he immediately became strong as in the days of his youth.

The king was very angry with the youngest son and sent him away with an officer who was skilled in the forest. The officer was a friend of the young prince and helped him to find a safe hiding-place, where he lived a long time.

By and by the three great kings came from distant lands with many presents for the prince who had given them peace and great prosperity. They told the father what a wonderful son he had, and wanted to give him their thanks. The father called the officer whom he had sent away with the young man and acknowledged the wrong he had done. The officer told him the prince was not dead, so the king sent messengers to find him.

Meanwhile one of the most beautiful princesses of all the world had sent word everywhere that she would be seated in her house and any prince who could walk straight to her along a line drawn in the air by her sorcerers, without turning to either side, should be her husband. There was a day set for the contest.

The messengers sent out by the king to find the prince knew all about this contest, so they made all things known to their young chief when they found him. He went with his swift steps of love to the land of the beautiful girl. His brothers had both failed in their most careful endeavors, but the young prince followed his heart's desire and went straight to a door which opened of its own accord. Out leaped the maiden of the palace of the land of Ka-ne. Into his arms she rushed and sent her servants everywhere to proclaim that her lord had been found.

The brothers ran away to distant lands and never returned. The prince and the princess became king and queen and lived in great peace and happiness, administering the affairs of their kingdom for the welfare of their subjects.

Chapter 7

MAMALA THE SURF-RIDER

"Kou" was a noted place for games and sports among the chiefs of long ago. A little to the east of Kou was a pond with a beautiful grove of coconut-trees belonging to a chief, Hono-kaupu, and afterward known by his name. Straight out toward the ocean was the narrow entrance to the harbor, through which rolled the finest surf waves of old Honolulu. The surf bore the name "Ke-kai-o-Mamala" (The sea of Mamala). When the surf rose high it was called "Ka-nuku-o-Mamala" (The nose of Mamala).

Mamala was a chiefess of kupua character. This meant that she was a mo-o, or gigantic lizard or crocodile, as well as a beautiful woman, and could assume whichever shape she most desired. One of the legends says that she was a shark and woman, and had for her husband the shark-man Ouha, afterward a shark-god having his home in the ocean near Koko Head. Mamala and Ouha drank awa together and played konane on the large smooth stone at Kou.

Mamala was a wonderful surf-rider. Very skilfully she danced on the roughest waves. The surf in which she most delighted rose far out in the rough sea, where the winds blew strong and whitecaps were on waves which rolled in rough disorder into the bay of Kou. The people on the beach, watching her, filled the air with resounding applause, clapping their hands over her extraordinary athletic feats.

The chief, Hono-kau-pu, chose to take Mamala as his wife, so she left Ouha and lived with her new husband. Ouha was angry and tried at first to injure Hono and Mamala, but he was driven away. He fled to the lake Ka-ihi-Kapu toward Waikiki. There he appeared as a man with a basketful of shrimps and fresh fish, which he offered to the women of that place, saying, "Here is life [i.e., a living thing] for the children." He opened his basket, but the shrimps and the fish leaped out and escaped into the water.

The women ridiculed the god-man. As the ancient legendary characters of all Polynesia could not endure anything that brought shame or disgrace upon them in the eyes of others, Ouha fled from the taunts of the women, casting off his human form, and dissolving his connection with humanity. Thus he became the great shark-god of the coast between Waikiki and Koko Head.

The surf-rider was remembered in the beautiful mele, or chant, coming from ancient times and called the mele of Hono-kau-pu:

"The surf rises at Koolau,
  Blowing the waves into mist,
  Into little drops,
  Spray falling along the hidden harbor.
  There is my dear husband Ouha,
  There is the shaking sea, the running sea of Kou,
  The crab-like moving sea of Kou.
  Prepare the awa to drink, the crab to eat.
  The small konane board is at Hono-kau-pu.
  My friend on the highest point of the surf.
  This is a good surf for us.
  My love has gone away.
  Smooth is the floor of Kou,
  Fine is the breeze from the mountains.
  I wait for you to return,
  The games are prepared,
  Pa-poko, pa-loa, pa-lele,
  Leap away to Tahiti
  By the path to Nuumealani (home of the gods,)
  Will that lover (Ouha) return?
  I belong to Hono-kau-pu,
  From the top of the tossing surf waves.
  The eyes of the day and the night are forgotten,
  Kou has the large konane board.
  This is the day, and to-night
  The eyes meet at Kou."

Chapter 8

A SHARK PUNISHED AT WAIKIKI

Among the legendary characters of the early
Hawaiians was Ka-ehu—the little yellow shark
of Pearl Harbor. He had been given magic power
and great wisdom by his ancestor Ka-moho-alii
the shark-god, brother of the fire goddess Pele.
Part of his life had been spent with his parents,
who guarded the sea precipices of the Coast of
Puna in the southern part of the island Hawaii.
While at Pearl Harbor he became homesick for
the beauty of Puna, so he chanted:

"O my land of rustling lehua*-trees!
  Rain is treading on your budding flowers,
  It carries them to the sea.
  They meet the fish in the sea.
  This is the day when love meets love,
  My longings are stirring within me
  For the spirit friends of my land.
  They call me back to my home,
  I must return."

* Ohia-lehua.   Metrosideros polymorpha.

Ka-ehu called his shark friends and started along the Oahu shores on his way to Hawaii. At Waikiki they met Pehu, a shark visitor from Maui, who lived in the sea belonging to Hono-ka-hau. Pehu was a man-eating shark and was swimming back and forth at Kalehua-wike.* He was waiting for some surf-rider to go out far enough to be caught.

Ka-ehu asked him what he was doing there. He replied, "I am catching a crab for my breakfast."

Ka-ehu said, "We will help you catch your crab."

He told Pehu to go near the coral reef while he and his large retinue of sharks would go seaward. When a number of surf-riders were far out he and his sharks would appear and drive them shoreward in a tumultuous rush; then Pehu could easily catch the crab. This pleased the shark from Maui, so he went close to the reef and hid himself in its shadows.

Ka-ehu said to his friends: "We must kill this man-eating shark who is destroying our people. This will be a part of our pay to them for honoring us at Puu-loa (Pearl Harbor). We will all go and push Pehu into the shallow water."

* Near the Moana Hotel.

56

A number of surf-riders poised on the waves, and Pehu called for the other sharks to come, but Ka-ehu told him to wait for a better chance. Soon two men started on a wave from the distant dark blue sea where the high surf begins.

Ka-ehu gave a signal for an attack. He told his friends to rush in under the great wave and as it passed over the waiting Pehu, crowd the men and their surf-boards to one side and push the leaping Pehu so that he would be upset. Then while he was floundering in the surf they must hurl him over the reef.

As Pehu leaped to catch one of the coming surf-riders he was astonished to see the man shoved to one side, then as he rose almost straight up in the water he was caught by the other sharks and tossed over and over until he plunged head first into a deep hole in the coral. There he thrashed his great tail about, but only forced himself farther in so that he could not escape.

The surf-riders were greatly frightened when they saw the company of sharks swimming swiftly outside the coral reef—but they were not afraid of Pehu. They went out to the hole and killed him and cut his body in pieces. Inside the body they found hair and bones, showing that this shark had been destroying some of their people.

They took the pieces of the body of that great fish to Pele-ula,* where they made a great oven and burned the pieces.

Ka-ehu passed on toward Hawaii as a knight-errant, meeting many adventures and punishing evil-minded residents of the great sea.

* Near corner Nuuanu and Beretania Streets.

Chapter 9

THE LEGENDARY ORIGIN OF KAPA

Note: **Dr. Brigham, the director of the Bishop Museum in Honolulu, well says, "Kapa (tapa) is simply ka (the) and pa (beaten) or the beaten thing."**

The cloth used for centuries by the Hawaiians and some other Polynesians was "the beaten thing" resulting from beating the inner mucilaginous bark of certain trees into pulp and then into sheets which could be used for clothing or covering.

The letters "k" and "t" have from time immemorial been interchangeable among the Hawaiians, therefore the words "kapa" and "tapa" have both been freely used as the name of the ancient wood-pulp cloth of the Hawaiians.

The old people said that in the very long ago their ancestors did not have anything like the kapa cloth which has been known for many centuries. They said also that there was no kapa maoli, meaning that there was nothing in nature which provided clothing or covering. Very little reference is made in the legends to the use of skins as clothing, although the dog and pig were brought with chickens by their early ancestors.

The clothing of the oldest time was sometimes made by tying dried banana leaves around the body, and coverings were made by throwing dry banana leaves over the body. Thus Kawelo was warmed and brought back to life, according to one of the most famous legends of the island Kauai.

The long, fragrant leaves of the ti* plant were dried, soaked in water until soft, the outside scraped off, then fastened together by braiding or tying. In this way a very warm cloak was made and worn by bird-catchers. They found it very good for shedding rain and keeping out cold when they went into the mountains.

Sometimes the long leaves of the Lau-hala were thatched into covering for the body as well as for the house. So also grass was braided into very fine cloaks as well as into mats. Banana leaves hanging in strips like a fringe were used for malos (loin cloths) for men, and pa-us (skirts) for women.

For many generations the Hawaiians made most beautiful and costly feather garments.

* Cordyline terminalis.

They braided or wove a foundation mesh of very fine vegetable fibres, such as the long threads of the ieie† vine. This mesh was fashioned into a mahiole, or warrior's helmet, a kihei, or shoulder cape, or an ahuula, or long cloak, and covered with the most brilliant red and golden feathers which could be secured from the birds of the forest.

In the legend of Makuakaumana the gods Kane and Kanaloa are represented as feeling pity for one of their worshippers when they saw him shivering in a fierce storm of cold rain; therefore they taught him how to make a kihei, or shoulder cape. Great was the wonder of the people of the northern side of the island of Oahu when he appeared among them and taught them how to make cloaks like "the gift of the gods." The legend is interesting, but only shows that the people sometime learned how to make a work-day cloak. Presumably the Hawaiian method of pounding the adhesive bark of certain trees until that bark becomes a pulpy mass and then making it into sheets and drying it was used in Samoa and many other islands of the Pacific Ocean and also even in Mexico hundreds of years ago. Evidently the Hawaiian brought the art with him or learned it from the sea rovers of about the tenth century. Nevertheless, the

† Freycinetii Arnotti.

Hawaiian legend of the origin of kapa is a myth well worth keeping on record in Hawaiian literature. It was partly published in a native paper, the *Kuokoa*, in 1865, but many references in other legends printed about the same time fill out the story.

Back of Honolulu a beautiful valley rises in a gentle slope between two rugged, precipitous ranges of lava mountains until it reaches cloudland and drinks ceaselessly from the fountains of the sky. A stream of laughing water rising from waterfalls blown into spray by swift winds rushes and leaps in numberless cascades through pleasant groves down this valley of restful shadows until it is lost in the coral reefs of an iridescent sea.

This is the noted Nuuanu Valley of winding ways loved by sightseers as they climb to the grand outlook over extinct craters, island coast and boundless ocean, called "the view from Nuuanu Pali."

This was the valley supposed to have been the first habitation of the gods, from which all life spread over the island group. Here the gnomes, or the eepa people, had their home, and here the Menehunes (the fairies) built a temple for "the child adopted by the gods."

The waters of the valley stream fertilized large areas where the valley broadened into the broad seaside plain in which now lies the city of Honolulu. Here at Pu-iwa, by the side of the running water, a farmer by the name of Maikoha lived with his daughters, having no care except raising whatever food they needed for themselves and for their tribute to the king and their offerings to the gods.

Years passed by and Maikoha became weak and ill. The eepa people of the upper valley had always sent driving rains and cold winds down the valley, and Maikoha had cared little for them; but the old man at last went into the days of death feeling a chill which struck to his very heart. On his death-bed he called his daughters and commanded them to listen carefully and to obey his words, saying: "When I die, bury my body close to the waters of our pleasant stream. A tree will grow from that burial-place. This tree will be to you for kapa, from which you will make all things good for clothing as well as covering when you sleep or are ill. The bark of this tree is the part you will use."

When death came, the daughters buried their father by the running water. After a time a tree grew from the grave. The daughters saw that it was a new tree such as they had never seen before. It was not tall and large, but threw out a number of small, spreading branches. This was the wauke* tree.

The daughters with great fear drew near to this monument which was over their father's grave. They believed it was a gift from the aumakua, the ghost-god, into which they supposed the spirit of their father had been changed.

Reverently they touched the tree, broke off some of the branches, stripped off the bark, and pounded and pounded until the pieces were fastened together in a rude kind of cloth. Thus they found kapa, "the beaten thing," and learned how to make it into small and large pieces and out of these fashion such clothing as met their need.

Wherever they cut or broke the branches of this new tree the broken pieces took root, or, if the fragments were caught by the swift-flowing stream, they were tossed on the bank or carried and scattered over the plain, and wherever they went they found a place to plant themselves until they grew even to the sea.

Branches were carried to the other islands; thus the wauke became a blessing to all the people. This tree under the name "aute," which is the same as wauke, was a blessing to many Polynesians, from Tahiti to New Zealand.

* Broussonetia papyrifera.

64

In after years other trees, such as the mamaki,* the maa-loa and po-ulu, were found to have bark from which kapa could be made; but the old people said, "From the wauke we get the best kapa for fine, soft clothing."

Maikoha became the chief aumakua, or ancestor-god, of the Hawaiian kapa-makers, and has been worshipped for generations. When they planted the wauke branches, or shoots, prayers and incantations and sacrifices were offered to Maikoha. Before branches were cut and placed in bundles to be carried to a field set apart for kapa-making, the favor of Maikoha was again sought.

One of the daughters of Maikoha, whose name was Lau-hu-iki, became the aumakua of all those who pounded the prepared bark, for to her was given the power of finding kapa in the bark of the wauke-tree, and she had the power of teaching how to pound as well as bless the labor of those who worshipped her.

The other daughter, Laa-hana, was also worshipped as an aumakua by those who used especially marked clubs while beating the bark into patterns or marked lines, for they said she learned how to scratch the clubs with sharks' teeth so that marks would be left in the pounded sheets. She was also able to teach those who

* Pipturus Albidus.

65

worshipped her to mark figures or patterns on the pounded kapa.

Thus Maikoha and his daughters became the chief gods of the kapa-makers; but other ancestral gods were also found from time to time as some new step was taken in perfecting the art.

Ehu, a man, was made the aumakua of kapa-dyers because he learned how to dip the cloth in dyes and give it color. He discovered the red dye in the blood of the kukui* tree; therefore prayers were offered to him and sacrifices laid on his altar when the kapa-maker desired to color some of the work.

A small corner in a house in the kapa-field usually had a very small pile of stones called "the altars." Here small offerings of leaves or fruit could be placed while the worshipper chanted his prayer.

Kapa-dyers searched forests for trees and plants which could give life-blood for different dyes. The sap of these plants was carefully put in bamboo joints and carried to the place where the pounders sang and worked.

Offerings of leaves and fruits and flowers were made to Ehu from time to time while the dyes were being collected as well as when they were used to color the kapa.

* Aluerites Moluccana.

Sometimes the sheets were spotted by sprinkling colors over them. Sometimes they were marked in lines and figures by using bamboo splints or bamboos with ends pounded into brush-like fibres. Stone cups were kept in the kapa-fields for the dye and the marking-splint.

Sometimes torn-up pieces of dyed kapas were pounded up with new sheets, producing a mottled effect. White kapas of the best texture were used in the temples to cover the gods during certain parts of the temple ceremonies. They were also used to mark a strict tabu. When kapa was laid on an object, it meant that it was not to be touched under pain of punishment by the guarding aumakua. Fastened to a staff and placed in a path, it meant that this path was tabu. It was in this way that tabu standards were placed around the temples.

A kapa dipped in a black dye was kept for the death covering, especially for those of very high rank.

Sometimes the perfumes of sweet flowers or the oil of such trees as the iliahi* (sandalwood) were pounded into the kapa while it was being made. The perfumes were made in this way. The sweet-smelling things were placed in a calabash and covered with water. Hot stones were put in the water and the fragrance drawn out of the

* Santalum Freycinetianum.

plants. The water was boiled away until the perfume became very strong. This was done with the sweet-scented flowers of the niu† (coconut) and of the lau-hala,‡ and the wood of the iliahi and other fragrant plants.

When the kapas were perfumed, they were dried inside a house so that the fragrance should not be lost.

Sometimes the kapas were well scraped with pieces of shell or rubbed with stones, then were rolled in dirt and put in a calabash and well soaked for a long time. When these kapas were washed, scraped and pounded again, they became very soft. Often the kapa-maker would take these sheets of kapa and spread them over a layer of cold, wet, fresh-water moss, leaving them all night for the dew to fall upon. These kapas became very bright and shining. Sometimes finished kapas were oiled so that they became excellent protectors from the wet and cold of heavy mists and rains. These oiled kapas were frequently varnished by being rubbed with eggs. Spider eggs were considered the best for this purpose.

In the early time a fiat stone was used upon which to pound out the sheets of kapa, but blocks of wood and long, heavy sticks were found to give the best results. These were called

† Cocos nucifera.   ‡ Pandanus adoratissimus.

kua-kuku. A block cut in a certain way was very much liked by the women, for it gave back a soft sound with the rhythmic beat of the mallets, accompanied by their own chants and incantations to Maikoha or one of the other aumakuas.

Hina, the mother of the demi-god Maui, was the great kapa-maker of the legends of the ancient Hawaiians. It is said that she still spreads her kapas in the sky. They are the beautiful clouds of all colors, sometimes piled up and sometimes lying in sheets. When fierce winds blow and lift and toss the cloud kapas and roll off the stones which Hina has placed on them to hold them down, or when she throws off the stones herself, the noise of the rolling stones is the thunder which men hear.

When Hina rolls the cloud sheets together, the folds glisten and flash in the light of the sun; thus what men call lightning is the sunlight leaping from sheet to sheet of Hina's kapas in cloudland.

Chapter 10

CREATION OF MAN

The Kamakau Legend

Note: Mauka* of Honolulu rises a cloud-capped range. Beyond this is the place where Kamakau, a native historian of about sixty years ago, says that the Hawaiian gods created the first inhabitants of these islands. The story has been repeated in several Hawaiian papers and with embellishments, was adopted by Judge Fornander and mentioned in notes in his work "The Polynesian Race." Parts of the story are evidently old Hawaiian, but the part which describes the creation of man is thoroughly Biblical with the addition of a few touches of the imagination.

"The sky is established.
The earth is established.
Fastened and fastened,
Always holding together,
Entangled in obscurity,
Near each other a group of islands
Spreads out like a flock of birds.
Leaping up are the divided places.
Lifted far up are the heavens.

* Toward the mountain.

70

Polished by striking,
Lamps rest in the sky.
Presently the clouds move,
The great sun rises in splendor,
Mankind arises to pleasure,
The moving sky is above."   *Hawaiian Chant.*

❋   ❋   ❋

Ku, Ka-ne, Lono and Kanaloa were the first gods made. The gods had come from far-off unknown lands. They brought with them the mysterious people who live in precipices and trees and rocks. These were the invisible spirits of the air.

The earth was a calabash. The gods threw the calabash cover upward and it became the sky. Part of the thick "flesh" became the sun. Another part was the moon. The stars came from the seeds.

The gods went over to a small island called Mokapu, and thought they would make man to be chief over all other things. Mololani was the crater hill which forms the little island. On the sunrise side of this hill, near the sea, was the place where red dirt lay mixed with dark blue and black soil. Here Ka-ne scratched the dirt together and made the form of a man.

71

Kanaloa ridiculed the mass of dirt and made a better form, but it did not have life. Ka-ne said, "You have made a dirt image; let it become stone."

Then Ka-ne ordered Ku and Lono to carefully obey his directions. They were afraid he would kill them, so at once they caught one of the spirits of the air and pushed it into the image Ka-ne had made.

When the spirit had been pushed into the body, Ka-ne stood by the image and called, "Hiki au-E-ola! E-ola!" ("I come, live! live!")

Ku and Lono responded "Live! live!" Then Ka-ne called again, "I come, awake! awake!" and the other two responded, "Awake! awake!" and the image became a living man.

Then Ka-ne cried, "I come, arise! arise!" The other gods repeated, "Arise! arise!" and the image stood up—a man with a living spirit. They named him Wela-ahi-lani-nui, or "The great heaven burning hot."

They chanted, giving the divine signs attending the birth of a chief:

Note: Fornander, in his book "The Polynesian Race," says that Lono brought whitish clay from the four ends of the world, with which to make the head, but there is no foundation for this statement in the legends. This must have been a verbal statement made to him by Kamakau.

"The stars were burning.
Hot were the months.
Land rises in islands,
High surf is like mountains,
Pele throws out her body (of lava).
Broken masses of rain from the sky,
The land is shaken by earthquakes,
Ikuwa* reverberates with thunder."

The gods took this man to their home and nourished him. When he became strong he went out to walk around the home of the gods. Soon he noticed a shadow going around with his body. It walked when he walked, and rested when he rested. He wondered what this thing was, and called it "aka," or "shadow."

When he slept, Ku, Ka-ne and Lono tore open his body, and Ka-ne took out a woman, leaving Ku and Lono to heal the body. Then they put the woman by the side of the man and they were alike.

Wela-ahi-lani-nui woke and found a beautiful one lying by him, and thought: "This is that thing which has been by my side, my aka. The gods have changed it into this beautiful one." So he gave her the name "Ke-aka-huli-lani" (The-heaven-changed-shadow). These were the ancestors of the Hawaiians and all the peoples of the islands of the great ocean.

* Ikuwa was the month of thunder and lightning.

It must be remembered that there are many other Hawaiian legends which mention other first men and women as ancestors of the Hawaiian people.

Chapter 11

THE CHIEF WITH THE WONDERFUL SERVANTS*

A certain chief who lived on the island of Oahu in the very misty memory of long, long ago thought he would travel over his lands and see their condition. So pleased was he that he boasted of his wide domain when he met a fellow-traveller. The man said, "I can see the lands of Wakea and Papa and they are larger and fairer than these fine places of yours." Then they decided to go together to find that wonderful land of the gods.

Soon they passed a man standing by the wayside. The chief asked him what he was doing. The man replied: "I am Mama-loa [The very swift]. I am waiting for the sun to rise, that I may run and catch him." They all waited until the sun appeared and started to rise above the island. The man ran very fast and caught it, fled it, and held it as a prisoner for a time.

* From the *Kuokoa* of 1862, Hawaiian newspaper.

75

Then the three travelled together—the chief, whose name was Ikaika-loa (The very strong), and the man who could see clearly a long distance, whose name was Ike-loa (The-far-sighted), and Mama-loa. In a little while they saw two men sleeping by the path. One was shivering with cold; his name was Kanaka-make-anu (Man-who-dies-in-the-cold). The other was burning as if over a fire; his name was Kanaka-make-wela (Man-who-dies-in-the-fire). They warmed one and cooled the other, and all went on together.

They came to a field for rat-shooting, and found a man standing with bow and arrow, shooting very skilfully. His name was Pana-pololei (The-straight-shooter). They asked him to go to the lands of Wakea and Papa, so he journeyed with them. By and by they found a man lying by the path with his ear to the ground. The chief asked him, "What are you doing?" He looked up and said, "I have been listening to the quarrel between Papa and Wakea." The man who was listening to their harsh words was Hoo-lohe-loa (The-man-who-could-hear-afar-off). They all journeyed on until they entered a land* more beautiful than any they had ever seen before.

The watchmen of that country saw six fine-looking men coming and with them a seventh

* The legends say that one of the homes of Wakea and Papa was the splendid country around Nuuanu Valley and Honolulu.

man, superior in every way. The report of the coming of these strangers was quickly sent to the chiefess who ruled the land under Wakea and Papa. She commanded her chief to take his warriors and meet these strangers and bring them to her house. There they were entertained. While they slept the chiefess gathered her people together until the enclosure around the houses was filled with people.

In the morning Ikaika-loa, the chief, said to the chiefess: "I have heard that you propound hard riddles. If I guess your riddles you shall become my wife." The chiefess agreed, took him out of the house, and said, "The man who is now my husband is standing by the door of the house of Wakea and Papa; where is the door of that house?" The chief turned to Ike-loa and secretly asked if he could see the door of Papa's house. He looked all around and at last said: "The door of that house is where the trunk of that great tree is. If you are strong and can break that tree you can find the door, because it is in one of the roots of that tree."

Then the chief went out to that tree and lifted and twisted the bark and tore away the wood, opening the door.

After this the chiefess said: "There are three dogs. One belongs to our high chief, Wakea; one to his wife, Papa; and one is mine. Can you point out the dog belonging to each of us?"

The chief whispered to his servant Hoo-lohe-loa, "Listen and learn the names of the dogs." So the man who could hear clearly put his ear to the ground and heard Papa telling her servants: "This black dog of Papa's shall go out first, then the red dog of Wakea. The white dog belonging to the chiefess shall go last." Thus the chief learned how to name the dogs.

When the black dog leaped through the door the chief cried out, "There is the black dog belonging to Papa."

When the red dog followed he said, "That is the red dog of Wakea."

Then came the white dog, and the chief cried out, "That white dog belongs to us, O Chiefess."

After this they prepared for a feast. The chiefess said: "Very far is the sweet water we wish. You send one of your men and I will send one of my women each with a calabash for water. If your man comes back first while we eat, we will marry."

The chief gave a calabash to Mama-loa and he made ready to go—a woman with her calabash standing by his side.

At the word they started on their race. The man ran swiftly, thinking there was no one among all men so swift as he, but the woman passed him and was leaving him far behind.

The chief called Pana-pololei, the straight shooter, and told him they needed his skill. He took his bow and arrows and shot. Far, far the arrow sped and whizzed just back of the head of the woman. She was so startled that she stumbled and fell to the ground and the man passed by.

After a time the chief said to Ike-loa, the far-sighted, "How are they running now?"

The servant said, "The woman is again winning."

The chief said to his rat-hunter, "Perhaps you have another arrow?" and again an arrow sped after the swift runners. It grazed the back of the woman and she fell. Mama-loa passed her, rushed to the spring, filled his calabash and started back. But the woman was very swift, and, quickly dipping her calabash, turned and soon passed the man. An arrow sped touching the head of the woman, and she fell forward, breaking the calabash and spilling the water; but she leaped up and saved a little water and hastened after the man who had sped past her.

"Ah, how she runs! She flies by the man as they are almost at the end of their race," exclaimed Ike-loa.

Then the chief called to his bowman: "O Pana-pololei! Perhaps you have another arrow?" The bowman shot a blunt arrow, striking the woman's breast, and she fell, out of breath, losing all the water from her broken calabash.

The chief took the calabash from his man and poured water into a coconut-cup and gave to the chiefess to drink.

When the woman came the chiefess asked why she had failed. The woman replied" "I passed that man, but something struck me and I fell down. This came to me again and again, but I could not see anything. At last I fell and the calabash was broken and all the water lost, and this man won the race."

Meanwhile Mama-loa was being ridiculed by the other servants of the chief. He asked: "Why do you laugh at me? Did you not see my victory?"

They laughed the more, and said: "Ka! If we had not aided you, you would have been defeated." Then they told him how he had been watched by the far-sighted one and aided by the arrows of his friend.

The chiefess told the chief that she had one more test before the marriage could take place.

She said: "In this land there are two places, one very hot and one very cold. If you can send men to live in these two places we will marry."

Then the chief said to Kanaka-make-anu, "You die in the cold, but perhaps you can go to the very hot place for the chiefess." And Kanaka-make-wela who suffered from heat he asked to go into the cold. The two servants said: "We go, but we will never return. These are our natural dwelling-places."

There were no more riddles to solve, so the chief and chiefess married and lived royally in that beautiful land of the gods.

Chapter 12

THE GREAT DOG KU

KU-ILIO-LOA

Ku, the dog-man, decided to come down from the clouds and visit mankind, so he assumed the form of a little dog and went around almost unnoticed.

Ku saw a group of three rainbows moving from place to place or resting for a long time above the home of a high chief. Sometimes the rainbows went up to the forests of ohia and kukui-trees on the mountain-side. Sometimes they rested over the deep pools made by the waterfalls of the swiftly descending mountain streams. Most frequently the beautiful colors were arched over a small grove of trees around a bathing-pool protected on two sides by steep ledges of rock over which diverging streams poured their cool waters which rose from the shadows and rippled away through the little valley toward the sea. On the remaining side of this sequestered nook was a sunny beach of black sand, back of which the trees opened their promise of refreshing shade.

Here Na-pihe-nui, the daughter of the high chief, came daily with her company of maidens to bathe and sport in the water and then let the afternoon hours pass in rest and pleasant conversation.

One day while diving into the pool from a shelf on the rocky ledge one of the girls saw something moving on the shore. She called to her companions and with them hastened to the place where their clothes had been thrown down. Here they found a little white dog lying on the kapa mantle of the princess.

For a time they played with the little stranger and were very much delighted with his unusual intelligence. He gambolled around them in great delight, obeying the call of one after the other, but showing very marked preference for the princess. When the maidens returned home they took the little dog with them and cared for him.

The high chief, Polihale, was interested in the peculiar powers possessed by this strange dog. Perhaps he thought that it was under the control of some spirit. His suspicions were in some way aroused and the dog was watched. Soon the chief learned that this was a man of marvellous ability, who could appear as a dog or a man at his own pleasure. Then the chief called his retainers and ordered them to kill this dog. They gathered stones and clubs and tried to surround it, but it dashed into the woods and made its escape. It was the great dog Ku, who had seen the three rainbows and followed them to the bathing-pool and then, having seen the princess, had determined to find an opportunity to carry her away as his wife. This premature discovery drove him away before he could accomplish his purpose.

Then Ku changed himself into a man of fine appearance and came boldly to the high chief's home demanding the princess in marriage, but the chief, warned by the omens as studied by his soothsayers, refused.

Ku was in great anger and threatened to kill the chief's people, and to destroy the protectors of the princess, but the high chief drove him away.

A dream came to the high chief, in which he saw the strange man coming as a great dog. The next morning as he looked toward the mountains he saw this same large dog stretching itself out of a cave on the mountain-side; so he knew that this dog with magical powers would be a very difficult enemy to overcome.

The chief soon learned that Ku was catching his people one by one and devouring them and decided to take final issue with his enemy.

Selecting a cave he hid all the women of his family in it, placing the princess in their care.

They took provisions with them and prepared for a long siege. Water could be found in the cave itself. Stones were placed before the opening so that the enemy would find it hard to enter.

Then the high chief and his followers waged war against Ku, the dog-man, but Ku was very strong and overthrew his pursuers when they closed in around him. Many times he killed some of the chief's people and carried their bodies away to feast upon them. He was also very swift in his motion, rapidly passing from place to place. Sometimes he fell like a flash of lightning upon a group of his foes and then in an incredibly short time he would make an attack in a far distant place.

The high chief became desperate and offered sacrifices to his gods and secured charms from his priests. Incantations and prayers were prepared against Ku.

At last a terrific battle was fought and Ku was overpowered and beaten to the ground. Still he fought fiercely, but the hard wooden spears pierced him and the heavy clubs broke his bones, until he lay a crushed and bleeding mass at the feet of his conquerors. Then they cut his body in two pieces, throwing one piece to one side and the other to a place some distance away. Then the power of the priests was invoked and the two parts of the body of Ku-ilio-loa became two great stones which have been objects of veneration among the Hawaiians for many years.

Ku stretches his form along the mountains and sometimes reveals himself as the great dog among the myriad shapes which the changing clouds are ever assuming. Sometimes he is seen in the clouds of Oahu, and then again his form is in the skies of other islands.

✳ ✳ ✳

Note: The Hawaiian legends frequently unite animal and human forms and characteristics in one individual, like the centaurs of Roman mythology. In some cases the man always carries with him a part of the animal shape. The legends of shark-men place the shark mouth between the shoulders of the man, and he is compelled to always wear a cloak to conceal his deformity.

Usually, however, the legends give to the human being the power to change at will into the peculiar animal form with which he has affinity without carrying with him any marks of his previous shape. In the Pele legends a chief appears as a beautiful bird and later as a handsome man, and marries the chiefess. When the hog-man Kamapuaa, however, courts Pele he is compelled to hide his pig-like deformities under a covering of kapa cloth.

The legend of the great dog Ku is somewhat reversed from the usual order. Ku, the dog, was given the power to change himself into a man and return into his animal form whenever he wished.

The legend is unique in that it unites a beautiful nature-myth with a history-myth of ferocious cannibalism.

Ku-ilio-loa is a magic dog who could be large or small at will. He roamed over the mountains and could be seen at night stretching himself from one peak to another or from the mountain height above his home in a cave below. This is evidently a nature-myth. The clouds on the mountains are ever multiform. Sometimes the dim mist in the moonlight rears its dog-shaped head over the sloping hills and stretches its shadowy length up to the faintly outlined peaks above; and sometimes the small cloud, like a dog at rest, lies quietly in the skies above the mountain forest. It was a beautiful outgrowth of Hawaiian imagination.

The same nature-myth has been applied to the cloud forms of lower Manoa Valley, a suburb of Honolulu. This cloud-myth was known as the story of Poki, the wonder-dog. He was often seen at night especially by those who had stood on the sacred bell rock of Kamoiliili. This rock rang with a sweet, strong tone when struck sharply. It had the power of giving clear vision to the one who stood on it and absorbed its mysterious qualities. The visitor must stand on the rock and utter his wish to see Poki. Then would his eyes be opened and the wonder-dog of the mountains of Oahu would reveal himself stretched along the mountains and silvered by the moonlight. Some of the later Hawaiians say that this wonder-dog of Oahu is the spirit of the chief Boki, who with his wife Liliha owned the lower part of the valley of Manoa. Bold in the early days of missionary labor in the Hawaiian Islands became desirous of seeing the world and adding to his riches; therefore he fitted out two ships for foreign trade and sailed away. The ship in which Chief Boki sailed was never heard from. Hence arose the saying, "We will do this or that when Boki comes back."

But some of the people changed the thought of the old legend and claimed that his spirit returned and now reveals himself as the dog watching over his loved valley. Magic powers were given to Poki—so that he could stretch himself along the mountains, his hind feet on the mountain ridge and his bead in the valley below. He could also extend himself to Nuuanu Valley and sometimes spread his body over all the island. Probably the only real connection of Chief Boki with the wonder-dog Poki is the similarity of names. But the chief has been almost forgotten. Even the wonder-dog is known only by the story-tellers, while the night clouds, sometimes darkened by falling rain, sometimes enriched by the halo of lunar rainbows, and sometimes glorified by the silver moonlight, continue to stretch from peak to peak along the mountains and watch over all the various forms of life in the valleys below.

Ku-ilio-loa, the great dog Ku, was destined to have another series of legends grow up about his memory besides those suggested by the adoring imaginations of nature lovers.

It is difficult to analyze the influences which brought the beautiful nature-myth down to the degradation of the sensuous life of a brute. Perhaps the simplest thought is the best, and the problem is solved by supposing that a chief by the name of Ku became imbued with cannibalistic desires and when driven away from his fellow-men made his home among the almost inaccessible peaks where cloud-myth and cannibal-legend could very easily be interwoven with each other as the memory of his horrible cannibal life became dimly connected with the mysterious cloud-forms among which he died.

89

Chapter 13

THE CANNIBAL DOG-MAN

Note: The Menehunes were the fairies of Hawaii. The goblins and gnomes of valley or woodland were called the eepa people, while monsters having the power of appearing in different kinds of bodies were called kupuas. These usually had cruel and vindictive characters and were ready to destroy and devour any persons they could catch. There were, however, many kupuas of kindly spirit who gave watchful care to the members of their own families.

The Menehunes were temple-builders, makers of great fish-ponds and even highways. They made canoes, built houses, and did many of the pleasant things fairies are always doing. Their good works are to be found to this day on all the different islands of the Hawaiian group.

※　　※　　※

Ka-hanai-a-ke-akua (The-adopted-child-of-the-gods) was the chief whose followers fought with the dragon-god, Kuna, for a canoe in Nuuanu

Valley. He was a friend of the fairies—the Menehune people. When he had grown into young manhood and was going to have a temple of his own, with his own gods to worship, the Menehunes heard about the plan for the walls and altars and determined to build that temple for the chief.

As soon as the night shadows had fallen over the mountains back of Honolulu the Menehunes were called together by their luna, or leader. The stones necessary for the heiau (temple) walls were pointed out. Flat-sided stones were selected for raised places and altars, smooth stones were called for from the seashore to be laid down as the temple floor. Bamboo and ohia sticks were to be brought with which to build platforms for sacrifices, such as the bodies of human victims. All parts of the temple building* even to the thatched houses for the priests and chiefs were portioned among the little people.

In one night the work was finished, a feast was eaten, and the Menehunes had scattered in the shadows of the forest thickets.

Kahanai took possession of his temple and dedicated it with the tabu service and ceremonies. This meant that a tabu of silence or a tabu forbidding work of any kind would be

---

* This heiau (temple) was on the road to Pauoa Valley, now Pacific Heights.

announced, and all the people of the district or place in which the temple was located would obey that tabu until the dedication ceremonies were all over and the words "Noa, ua noa" were used, meaning that the tabu was over and everything could be freely done as before.

The name given to this temple was Ka-he-iki. In this temple the chief placed his friend and guardian, Kahilona, who had cared for him from his babyhood, as his priest and teacher. Kahilona was the priest of this temple. Kahilona prepared this chant for the temple building.

> "Gone is the little house,
>   The little house,
>   Gone is the large house,
>   The large house,
>   Gone is the short house,
>   The short house,
>   Gone is the little house,
>   From Maiuu to Maaa-e.
>   Let this be commenced.
>
> Build, with the soft beat of the drum,
> With the murmur of the voice of the gods,
> With the low whine of the dog,
> With the low grunt of the pig,
> And the soft whispers of men.
>   Here am I, Kahilona,
>   The teacher of prayer,
>   Proclaimed by Kahilona."

A kupua who was a dog-man overthrew the government of Kahanai and became the ruling power between Nuuanu Valley and the sea. His own house and heiau were at Lihue,—a place toward the Waianae Mountains. This kupua never attacked or injured any members of the family of the very high chief or king of the island Oahu, but he was a cannibal, and many of the people were killed and eaten by him. He could appear at will either as a man or a dog.

His name was Kaupe. After he had eaten some of the people of Oahu he went over the water to eat the men of Maui, and then went on to Hawaii, where he captured the son of one of the high chiefs and carried him back to Oahu, putting him in the temple at Lihue to keep him there until the time came for a human sacrifice. Then the boy was to be killed and laid on a platform before the gods.

The father of that boy left Hawaii to follow him to Oahu, thinking there might be some way of saving his son. If he failed he could at least die with him. When the father came to Oahu he very quietly landed and looked for some one to give him aid. After a time he met Kahilona, the caretaker of the temple of the Menehunes, and told him all his trouble.

The priest taught the father the proper incantations by which he could get his boy away from the magic power of Kaupe, and save both himself and his boy. Then he also taught the father a prayer which he was to use if Kaupe should learn of their escape and pursue them.

At night he approached the temple at Lihue repeating the chant which Kahilona had taught him. He watched for the signs which the priest had told him would indicate the place where the boy was kept, and followed them carefully. He continually repeated his chant until he came inside the walls and found the dog asleep guarding the boy. The father slipped in, cautiously aroused the boy, and unfastened the cords which bound him. Then they quietly passed the dog, guarded by the incantation:

"O Ku! O Lono! O Ka-ne! O Kanaloa!
 Save us two. Save us two."

Thus they passed out of the temple and fled toward the temple Ka-he-iki.

While they were running a great noise was heard far behind them. The dog had been awakened, and had discovered the escape of his prisoner. Then rushing like a whirlwind around the temple he found the direction in which they had fled. This was the path naturally taken by those leaving Oahu to escape to Hawaii. The great dog only waiting to learn the course taken, pursued them on the wings of the wind.

The two chiefs fled, but saw that it was impossible to outrun the dog. Then the father uttered the prayer which the priest had said would save them if Kaupe followed. They ran with increased strength and swiftness, but the dog would soon be upon them. Again the father repeated the prayer:

"O Ku! O Lono! O Ka-ne! O Kanaloa!
  By the power of the gods,
  By the strength of this prayer,
  Save us two. Save us two."

Then they found a great stone at Moanalua under which they were able to hide.

The dog had only one thought, which was that the father and son would return to Hawaii as speedily as possible aided by their gods, so he rushed to the beach, leaped into the air and flew to Hawaii.

The chiefs went to the temple Ka-he-iki, and were gladly welcomed by the priest, Kahilona, who taught them the prayers by which they could overcome and destroy the dog-man.

After they were fully instructed they returned to their home on Hawaii and waged war against their enemy. They obeyed the directions of the priest and finally killed Kaupe.

But the ghost of Kaupe was not killed. He returned as a ghost-god to the highest part of

Nuuanu Valley, where in his shadow body he can sometimes be seen in the clouds which gather around the mountain-tops or come down the valley. Sometimes his cloud-form is that of a large dog, and sometimes he is very small, but there his ghost rests and watches over the lands which at one time he filled with terror.

Kahilona, the priest of the temple Ka-he-iki, became the ancestor of one of the greatest of the priestly clans of the islands—the Mo-o-kahuna (the priests of the dragon) class of Oahu, noted for their ability to read the signs of sky and sea and land.

Chapter 14

THE CANOE OF THE DRAGON

Koa-trees, out of which the finest and most enduring calabashes of the old Hawaiians were made, grew near the ocean's sandy shore, but the koa-trees from which canoes were carved and burned were, according to some wise plan of Providence, placed on rough precipitous mountain-sides or on the ridges above.

The fierce winds of the mountains and the habit of bracing themselves against difficulties made the koa-trees cross-grained and slow in growth. The koa was the best tree of the Hawaiian Islands for the curled, twisted, and hard-grained wood needed in canoes which were beaten by overwhelming surf waves, rolled over sandy beaches, or smashed against coral or lava reefs.

From the time the canoe was cut in the mountains and was dragged and rolled over lava beds or sent crashing down steep mountain-sides to the time it lay worn out and conquered by the decay of old age it was always ready to meet the roughest kind of life into which its maker and owner could force it to go.

The calabash used in the plains and in the mountains came from a tree grown in beautiful lines by the sea. The canoe came from the hard mountain-koa far from its final workshop. There were gods, sacrifices, ceremonies, priests and even birds in the rites and superstitions of the canoe-makers. Kupulupulu was the god of the koa forest. Any wanderer in the woods was in the domain of that god. It was supposed that every rustling footstep was heard by most acute ears, and every motion of the hand was watched by the sharpest eyes. Dread of the unseen and unheard made every forest rover tremble until he had made some proper offering and uttered some effective incantation.

The ceremony and the wages of the priest who went up the mountain to select a koa-tree for canoe-cutting were like this: First he found a fine-appearing tree which he thought would make the kind of canoe desired. Then he took out his fire-sticks and rubbed rapidly until he had sparks of fire in the wood-dust of his lower stick. He caught the fire and made a burning oven (imu), heated some stones, cooked a black pig and a chicken, and prepared food for a feast, and then prayed:

"O Kupulupulu—the god!
  Here is the pig,
  Here is the chicken,
  Here is food.

  O Kupulupulu!
  O Kulana wao!
  O Ku-ohia laka!
  O Ku waha ilo!
  Here is food for the gods."

The aumakuas, or spirits of ancestors, were supposed to join with the gods of the prayer in partaking of the shadow of the feast, leaving the substance for the canoe-makers.

After the offering and prayer the priests ate and then lay down to sleep until the next day. In the morning after another feast they began to cut the tree.

David Malo, in his "Hawaiian Antiquities," said that the priest took his stone axe and called upon the female deities of the canoe-cutters thus:

"O Lea and Ka-pua-o-alakai!
  Listen now to the axe.
  This is the axe which is to cut the tree for the canoe."

Another account says that when the canoe priest began to cut the tree and also as long as they were chopping it down they were talking to the gods thus:

"O Ku Akua! O Paapaaina!
 Take care while the tree is falling,
 Do not break our boat,
 Do not let the tree smash and crack."

When the tree began to tremble and its leaves and branches rustle, a tabu of silence was enjoined upon the workmen, that the tree itself might be the only one heard by the watching gods.

When the tree had fallen a careful watch was made for Lea, the wife of Moku-halii, the chief god of the canoe-carvers—those who hollowed out the canoe.

It was supposed that Lea had a double body— sometimes she was a human being and sometimes she appeared as a bird.

Her bird body was that of the Elepaio, a little bird covered with speckled feathers, red and black on the wings, the woodpecker of the Hawaiians.

"When she calls she gives her name 'E-le-pai-o, E-le-pai-o, E-le-pai-o!' very sweetly."

If she calls while the tree is being cut down and then flies gently down to the fallen tree and runs up and down from end to end, and does not touch the tree, nor bend the head over, striking the wood, then that tree is sound and good for a canoe.

But if the goddess strikes the tree here and there it is rotten and of no use, and is left lying on the ground.

David Malo, as translated by Dr. Emerson, says:

"When the tree had fallen the head priest mounted the trunk, axe in hand, and called out in a loud voice, 'Smite with the axe, and hollow the canoe! Give me my malo!'

The priest's wife would hand him a white ceremonial malo with which he girded himself—then walked along the tree a few steps and called out in a loud voice, 'Strike with the axe, and hollow it! Grant us a canoe!'

Then he struck a blow on the tree with the axe. This was repeated until he reached the point where the head of the tree was to be cut off. Here he wreathed the tree with the ieie vine, repeated a prayer, commanded silence, and cut off the top of the tree.

This done, the priest declared the ceremony performed and the tabu lifted.

Then the priests took their stone adzes, hollowed out the canoe on the inside, and shaped it on the outside until in its rough shape it was ready to be dragged by the people down to the beach and finished and polished for its work in the sea."

Ka-hanai-a-ke-Akua was a chief residing near Kou. He lived in the time when gods and men mingled freely with each other and every tabu chief was more or less of a god because of his high birth.

His priests went up Nuuanu Valley to a place on the side where forests covered a small valley running into the side hills of the larger and more open valley. Great koa-trees fit for canoe-making were found in this forest. However, this part of the valley belonged to the eepa people— the deformed or ill-shaped gnomes of woodland or plain. Sometimes they seemed to be crippled and warped in mind as well as in body. They could be kind and helpful, but they were often vindictive and quarrelsome. There were also ferocious mo-o, or dragon-gods, watching for prey. Travellers were destroyed by them. They sometimes appeared as human beings, but were always ready to become mo-os.

One of these gods came down to the place where the priests were cutting the koa canoe for the high chief. He watched the ceremonies and listened to the incantations while the tree was being cut down. He tried to throw obstacles in the way of the men who were steadily breaking chips from the tree-trunk. He directed the force of the wind sweeping down the valley against them. He sent black clouds burdened with heavy driving rain. He made discouraging

102

omens and sent signs of failure, but the priests persevered.

At last the tree fell and was accepted. It was speedily trimmed of its branches, cut roughly to the required shape and partly hollowed out. Then coconut ropes and vines were fastened around it, and the people began to pull it down the valley to the harbor of Kou.

As they started to drag the log over rough lava ridges outcropping along the valley-side they found their first effort checked. The log did not move down into the valley. Rather, it seemed to go up the hillside. The god caught one end and pulled back. Another mighty effort was put forth and the canoe and the god slipped over the stones and partly down the hillside. But the dragon-god braced himself again and made the canoe very heavy. He could not hold it fast and it came down to the men. It was very difficult to drag it through the forest of the valley-side or the thickets of the valley, so the men pulled it down into the rough, rocky bed of the little stream known as Nuuanu. It was thought that the flowing water would help the men and the slippery stones would hinder the god.

Down they went pulling against each other. The god seemed to feel that the struggle under such conditions was hopeless, so he let go of the canoe and turned to the flowing water.

Beautiful waterfalls and cascades abound all along the course of this mountain stream. It is fed by springs and feathery waterfalls which throw the rainfall from the tops of the mountains far down into the valley.

The god hastened along this water course, stopped up the springs, and turned aside the tributary streams, leaving the bed of the river dry. Then he went down once more, caught the canoe, and pulled back. It was weary, discouraging work, and the chief's people became very tired of their struggle. The night fell when they were still some distance from the sea.

They had come to a place known as Ka-ho-o-kane.* In this place there were sharp turns, steep banks and great stones. Here the dragon-god fought most earnestly and wedged the log fast in the rocks.

The task had become so difficult and it was so dark that the high chief allowed his priests to call the people away, leaving the log in the place where the last struggle was made. It was a gift to the mo-o, the dragon, and was known as "The canoe of the dragon-god." It is said that it lies there still, changed into a stone, stuck fast among the other huge stones among which the water from the mountains finds its way laughing at the defeat of the canoe-makers.

* This place is in the heart of modern Honolulu back of the old Kaumakapili church site.

Chapter 15

THE WONDERFUL SHELL

Near Niolapa, on the eastern side of Nuuanu Valley, is the stone where Kapuni rested when he came after the shell known as the Kiha-pu. Kapuni was a child of Kauhola, who was said to have been a chief, who was born, was walking and had grown up, had become a father, a grandfather, and had died, all in one day. Kapuni was born in Waipio Valley, and was placed in the temple Pakaaluna and was made a god.

Two gods came from Puna. They were Kaakau and Kaohuwalu. They waited above Hakalaoa looking down into Waipio. There they saw Kapuni leaping. He touched a branch of a kukui-tree and fell down. He leaped again and touched the short top branches of the kukui and fell down.

Kaakau said to Kaohuwalu, "Suppose we get Kapuni to go with us as our travelling companion, one with us, in fierce storms, or in the cold heavy dews of night."

Kaohuwalu assented, and they arose and went down. They called to Kapuni, asking him to leap up. He tried again and again and always fell back.

Kaakau caught him as he fell and cut off part of his body because he was too heavy, then he could fly to the sky and return again.

Kaakau asked him how he was succeeding. He replied, "Very well indeed; I am swift in flight." Then Kaakau said, "Will you go with us on a journey?" Kapuni said, "Yes."

They went away to the lands of Kahiki and returned to Kauai. From there they heard the wonderful voice of a shell sounding from the temple Waolani in Nuuanu Valley.

Kapuni said, "What is that thing which makes such a sound?"

Kaakau said, "That is a shell which belongs to the eepas [gnomes], the people of Waolani, Oahu."

"I want that shell very much," said Kapuni. Kaakau told him that the task would be very difficult and dangerous, for the shell was guarded by watchmen from hill to hill, from the sea to the summit of the valley, and along all the pathways to the neighboring villages.

The gods, however, crossed the channel to Oahu, and rested at night above Kahakea. Here was a temple above Waolani. It was upon a hill. In it was a noted drum. The name of that temple was Pakaaluna. Kapuni told his friends to stay there waiting for him. If he did not return before the red dust of the dawn was in the sky they would know he was dead. If he returned he would have the shell.

Then he approached the prison enclosure outside the temple. Here he waited by a rock for all the watchmen on the high places around the temple to fall asleep. When the stars arose in the heavens above Nuuanu and all were sound asleep he entered the temple and took the shell. He flew away and found his companions.

They made a great jump and leaped to Kalaau Point. As they flew over the water to Molokai the shell touched the top of a wave and sang with a clear voice.

The god of Waolani Temple heard the shell singing, looked, and found that it had been stolen. He rushed from the temple, flew over the Nuuanu precipice and out into the channel from which he had heard the sound.

Kapuni hid among the waves, the shell ceased its song. The god of Waolani went back and forth over the water, but could find nothing.

After the god gave up the search Kapuni went on to Molokai and then to Maui and Hawaii. As it flew across the channel between Maui and Hawaii the shell struck a high wave and broke off a corner.

When they were on the hills of Hawaii they found the temple built at Hainoa. There the gods of Hawaii were gathered together.

Kiha was high chief of Hawaii at that time, and had been dwelling in Waipio Valley, cultivating his plant, planting awa, and building a temple for his gods.

When that temple was finished and the tabu of silence lifted from all the surrounding country he went to Kawaihae and built another temple, establishing another altar for his gods. He placed the usual tabu upon all the land around Kawaihae.

But the tabu was broken by the sound of that shell blown by the gods of the Hainoa Temple. He was very much troubled, but the gods were too strong for him. At last help came to him from Puapualenalena (The yellow flower), a dog belonging to a master who had left his home in Niihau some time before.

Puapualenalena was seeking his master, and found him on the uplands of Hawaii.

The dog excelled in his skill as a thief, stealing pigs, chickens, tapa cloth, all kinds of property for his master.

The master told that dog to get the tabu awa roots of the king, which were growing on the hillsides of Waipio Valley.

When that place was stripped, he sent the dog to the precipices of Waimanu, and he took nearly all that was there.

Then the king commanded his people to watch the awa fields and catch the one who was stealing his growing awa.

They began their watch. When the night was almost over and the dawn was touching the sky they found the thief. These men followed the thief and caught his master in a cave, all wrinkled from drinking much awa.

They took the master and the dog to the king Kiha as prisoners, and the king planned to have them steal that shell which troubled him. If they failed they should be put to death. This was the sentence of the king upon his prisoners.

The master talked with his dog, and told him all the word of the king. They planned to pay for the theft of the awa, but not by the death of their bodies.

The dog went out to win the shell from the gods under cover of the night, when the darkness was great and all kinds of shell voices were mingling with other voices of the woodland and wilderness.

Then came the softly resonant voice of that shell blown by the gods. According to an ancient chant, "The song of Kiha-pu calls

Kauai," meaning the song is listened to from far distant Kauai.

The dog ran swiftly while the sound of the shell was great, and hid in a corner of a stone wall of the heiau. He waited and waited a long time. The dawn was almost at hand. Then the watchers fell into deep sleep.

The dog crept softly inside, seized the shell and slipped it away from its place, then leaped over six walls of the heiau, but touched the seventh and outside wall. Then the shell sang out loud and clear.

The gods were aroused. They followed, but the dog leaped into a pool of water and concealed himself and the shell while the gods dashed by. They searched the road toward Waipio, then rushed toward the Kona district.

The dog flew from the pond down the precipice of Waipio Valley and laid the shell at the feet of Kiha, the king of Hawaii.

The dog and his master were given a high place in the affections of the king.

The shell was renowned for its wonderful sound, and could call the warriors of the king from any distance when the king caused it to be blown. It was known as Kiha's shell, the Kiha-pu.

This shell was carefully preserved by the chiefs of Hawaii from that ancient time. Generation after generation it was cared for. In the time of Kamehameha III. it was kept in his palace. It was among the treasures of King Kalakaua, and now has its resting-place in the hands of ex-Queen Liliuokalani in Honolulu.

When Kapuni died, his bones, worshipped as one of the gods, were kept at Kaawaloa until the tabu and the temples were overthrown.

Chapter 16

THE GHOST DANCE ON PUNCHBOWL

KA HULA O NA AUMAKUA

Punchbowl lies back of Honolulu. It is an extinct volcano. Inside the crater rim is a basin whose sides are grass-covered, with groups of trees here and there. The little houses and small gardens of squatters show that there is no longer any fear of subterranean activity. A large part of the city of Honolulu is built on what were once the brown, desolate sides of the volcano sloping down to the sea.

Punchbowl is one of the last attempts of the goddess of fire to retain her hold on the island of Oahu. The great ridge of mountains which forms the backbone of the island is a gigantic remnant of volcanic action, but the craters out of which this vast mass of lava was poured died centuries before the foothill craters threw out the last black sand of Punchbowl or uplifted the coral and the white sea sand and shells of Leahi Diamond Head.

In the indefinite long ago, Kakei was the moi, or high ruling chief, of Oahu. He was enterprising and brave. He not only perfected himself in the use of the spear, the war-club and the sling-stone, but he rallied around him the restless young chiefs of the districts which acknowl-edged his supremacy. His court was filled with men who gave and received blows, who won and lost in the many games, who were penniless today and rich to-morrow, and yet took all that came as a matter of course. Kakei called these younger chiefs together and told them to return to their districts for a time and make prepara-tions for a voyage and a battle. They must see that many new canoes were made and the best of the old ones repaired and repolished. They must select the bravest and best of their retain-ers and have them well armed and well provi-sioned. He hinted that it might be a long jour-ney, therefore they had better provide strong mat sails for all the canoes. It might be many days, therefore the provisions should be such as would last. At once the young men with great joy hastened to their homes to obey the will of their chief.

It was impossible to keep the people from talking about the expedition. Excitement pre-dominated. The shrill voices of the women shouted the news from valley to valley. The hum of unwonted industry was heard over all the island. Imagination was keenly intent to discover the point threatened by the proposed excursion. Night after night the people discussed the various enemies of their king, and his prospects for successful battle with them, or they talked of the enlargement of his kingdom by the acquisition of Molokai or the increase of riches by a foray along the coasts of Hawaii. They prophesied great victories and much spoil. Months passed by and all the preparations were complete. A splendid body of warriors were gathered around their high chief. The large flotilla of canoes was launched, the sails set, and the colored pennants placed at the end of each mast. The young chiefs were brilliant in their bright yellow and red war capes and hideous with the war masks which many of them proudly wore as they leaped into their canoes and shouted "Aloha" to the friends whom they were leaving.

As soon as the boats had left the shore the chief turned to the north rather than to the south, as all had been led to believe would be the course. Sails and paddles were both used freely. The winds of the seas and the strong arms of the oarsmen vied with each other in hastening the fleet toward the island of Kauai. Night crept over the waters, but the bright stars were unclouded and the path over the waters was as straight by night as it had been by day.

The morning star was shining and the dawn was painting the clear sky with wonderful tints of pearl when Kakei and his army of warriors, already on the land, raised their war-cry and assaulted the people of the village of Waimea.

Catching war-club and spear the chief of Waimea rushed out of his house, raising his war-cry. His men, half-awake, confused and dazed by the sudden attack, attempted to aid him in resisting the invaders. The battle was short and decisive. In a very little while many people were killed. The thatched houses were set on fire and a great destruction wrought.

Kakei had ordered his warriors to seize the canoes and the women and children and whatever plunder in calabashes, mats, kapa cloth, stone implements and feather cloaks could be had, and gather all together on the beach.

The captured canoes and their own great fleet were filled and the return safely made to Oahu. Kakei and his warriors sailed around the island to Honolulu Harbor. There the beach was covered with the new riches and the captive women and children. The king ordered a great feast to be prepared on the slopes of Punchbowl. Fish in abundance were caught, pigs and chickens were slaughtered, many ovens with red-hot stones were made ready, and huge calabashes of awa prepared.

Kakei and his victorious warriors gathered around the poi-bowl, while the hula-girls danced most joyously before them.

Suddenly the earth shook under them, the poi-bowls rocked as if tossed on the waters of the sea, the feast which had been spread before them moved from place to place as if made of things of life. The rocky cliffs of Punchbowl began to separate and come crashing down the hillside in great masses. The people fled in every direction, leaving a part of their number crushed under the failing stones.

Then came another mighty earthquake. The side of Punchbowl opened and a flood of lava poured out, mixed with clouds of steam and foul gases. Down over the place where the feast was spread on the luau mats poured the fire. The feast became the food of the fire-goddess. Then a wonderful thing appeared above the flowing lava, in the midst of the clouds hovering over the crater. A number of the aumakua of Kauai were seen in a solemn and stately dance. Back and forth they moved to the rhythm of steady peals of erupting gases. The clouds swayed to and fro, while the ghosts moved back and forth among them. The spirits of the ancestors had come to protect the women and children of the households whose friendly deities they were. It was the ceremonial, sacred dance

116

of the spirits, to be followed by swift punishment of those who had brought such great
injury to Kauai.

But while the ghosts continued their awful
dance, the terrified king and his warriors hastily prepared a propitiation. The captured
women and children were called to the beach.
All the plunder brought from Waimea was
hastily collected and placed in the hands of the
captives. The kahunas, the priests of the king,
were sent to the slope above Punchbowl Hill to
cry out to the aumakuas that all the reparation
possible would be made at once.

The warriors placed the captives and their
goods in canoes, and started back to Kauai. As
the canoes passed out of sight the earthquakes
ceased. No longer was there the thunder of
imprisoned gases leaping to liberty. The fires
died away, and the flood of lava cooled. The
aumakuas had accepted the offered repentance
of the king and his warriors.

It is said that the fire never again returned to
that crater or to the island of Oahu.

❖　　❖　　❖

Note: Curious and weird tales are told concerning these two small, picturesque volcanoes of

the city which in tropical luxuriance is one of the most beautiful spots in the Pacific Ocean. Near the foot of Diamond Head, and not far from the caves which burrow its sides, was the heiau (temple) which was one of the last to be glutted with human sacrifices. Its altars were loaded with bodies of dead men when Kamehameha brought his warriors from Hawaii and Maui and with much bloodshed conquered Oahu and unified the Islands under one government. On the brow of Diamond Head, fronting the sea, are the remains of a small fish-god temple within the walls of which the less cruel offerings were made to Kuula to gain his favor in securing food from the sea. Battles were fought and noted deeds of daring done both east and west of this prominent crater.

The summit of Punchbowl is crowned with a bold, frowning pile of perpendicular rocks. On the top of this pile peculiar human sacrifices are said to have been offered from time to time.

The natives whisper a story that one of the last kings of the Kamehameha family, in a drunken fit, so seriously injured his son that ultimately death resulted. The crazed father planned an expiation. The word was quietly passed that no one was to move far away from his home that night. There was an air of mystery around the city. What happened was never accurately known, but a fire burned on the high rock, and the smoke fell around it that night. It was hinted that a drunken sailor might easily have disappeared while staggering through the dark shadows, and be but little missed.

But back in the olden time there was laid the foundation for a legend which in these later days becomes a good folk-lore tale. Many of the Hawaiians of to-day believe in the continual presence of the aumakuas, the spirits of the dead. In time past the aumakuas were a powerful reality. An ancestor, a father or a grandfather, a makua, died. Sometimes he went to Po, the under-world, or to Milu, the shadow-land, or to Lani, the Hawaiian heaven, and sometimes he remained to be a torment or a blessing to his past friends.

In Samoa, Turner says that the aumakuas were supposed to come back from the underworld and enter into the bodies of those they wished to trouble. They might find a home in the stomach or heart or bowels, but wherever they found an abiding-place the spirit produced disease and death. If a man was dying, his neighbors desired to be on good terms with him and did all they could to make him comfortable.

This is very much like the power of praying to death among the Hawaiians. The spirit of some dead person was supposed to be the real destructive agent in putting to death the one prayed against. The aumakua (the ancestor spirit) was more powerful than any living human force.

In Tahiti the oro-matuas (aumakuas) were very malignant, cruel and relentless in punishing those who incurred their displeasure. In all the different groups of islands, however, the ghosts were supposed to belong to particular families and to exert their mysterious power in caring for these households. Many Hawaiian families have stories which are still firmly believed, of special favors granted to individuals in time of danger. A school-boy in Hilo told the writer how his grandfather was saved when his canoe upset, and how he was safely brought to the land by the shark into which the family aumakua had entered. The story is told of a man captured in battle, tied up in green ti leaves ready to be put into the pit full of red-hot stones, and then set free by the owl in which the protector of his family was dwelling. "People sometimes gave the bodies of their relatives to sharks in order that their spirits might enter into the sharks, or threw them into the crater of Kilauea, that the spirits might join the company of volcanic deities and afterward befriend the family."

Chapter 17

THE BIRD-MAN OF NUUANU VALLEY

Namaka was a noted man of the time of Kalaniopuu. He was born on Kauai, but journeyed forth to find some one whom he would like to call his lord. He was skilled in managing land (Kalai-aina), an orator (Kakaolelo), and could recite genealogies (Kaauhau). He excelled in spear-throwing (lonomakaihe), boxing or breaking the back of his opponent (lua), leaping or flying (lele) and astronomy (kilo). All this he had learned on Kauai.

Sailing from Kauai he landed on Oahu. In Nuuanu Valley he met Pakuanui, a very skilful man, a fine orator and boxer. He was the father of Ka-ele-o-waipio, a noted man of the time of Kamehameha, the maker of a chant for the missionaries at Kailua.

Toward the upper end of Nuuanu Valley, in a place Ka-hau-komo, where spreading hau* trees cluster on both sides of the road, Namaka and Pakuanui had a contest. They prepared them-

* Paritium tiliaceus.

121

selves for boxing and wrestling, and then faced each other to show their skill and agility.

This man from Kauai appeared like a rainbow bending over the hau-trees, arched in the red rain, or in the mist cloud over the Pali, as he circled around Pakuanui. He was like the ragged clouds of Lanihuli, or the wind rushing along the top of the Pali. His hands were like the rain striking the leaves of the bushes of Malailua. He was so swift and strong that he could catch Pakuanui in any part of his body.

The man of Oahu could not hold Namaka. That Kauai man was as slippery as an eel, and as hard to hold as certain kinds of smooth, slimy fish, always escaping the hands of Pakuanui. But he could strike any place. The hill of the forehead he struck, ridge of the nose also. There was no place he could not touch. He rushed like a whirlwind around the man. However, he did not try to kill Pakuanui. He wished only to display his skill.

Pakuanui was very much ashamed and angry because he could not do anything with Namaka, and planned to kill him when they should reach the Pali (precipice of Nuuanu Valley), to which they were going after the boxing contest.

When they came to Kapili at the top of the Pali, a very narrow place, Pakuanui said to Namaka, "You may go before me."

Namaka passed by on the outside and Paku-anui gave him a kick, knocking him over the Pali, expecting him to be dashed to pieces on the rocks at the foot of the precipice.

But Namaka flew away from the edge of the Pali. The people who were watching said: "He went off. He flew off from the Pali like an Io bird, leaping into the air of Lanihuli, spreading out his arms like wings. When the strong wind twisted and whirled, Namaka was lifted like a kite by the wind, and hung among the kukui branches below a little waterfall which is on the western side of the precipice where a rivulet starts on its way to the ocean." Then he leaped to the ground and went away to Maui. At Pohakuloa, on Maui, Namaka leaped down some precipices, showing his strength and skill.

When Namaka came to Hawaii, Kalaniopuu was king. He liked him very much and hoped to have him as his lord.

❈   ❈   ❈

Note: The older natives sometimes recall this wonderful flight of the man from Kauai who was skilful in leaping and flying from the edge of precipices.

However, another man from Kauai was a favorite with the king. He knew Namaka, and was afraid that he might be supplanted when the king should learn about Namaka's wonderful powers, so he gave no welcome to Namaka, but turned him away.

Namaka went to Waimea and found Hinai, the high chief of that place, a near relative to Kalaniopuu. He told Hinai what he could do, and was made a favorite of the high chief.

He taught Hinai how to be very skilful in all his arts, and especially in leaping from precipices. He hoped that Hinai's skill would be noised abroad, and the king would hear and wish to have the teacher come to live with him.

Hinai became very proficient, and even wonderful, in standing on the edge of high precipices and leaping down unhurt. These places have been pointed out to the young people by their parents.

When the favorite of Kalaniopuu heard that there was a very skilful man from Kauai stopping with the high chief of Waimea, he told the king that an enemy from Kauai was in Waimea.

The king listened to this man and then he charged Namaka with trying to make his relative Hinai so skilful in leaping down high places that he could always escape any attempt to injure him.

The favorite said: "This man, Namaka, can fly over mountains and streams and precipices and plains and not be killed. He is a rebel against your kingdom."

Kalaniopuu commanded some men to go and kill this stranger from Kauai, telling them to begin war upon Hinai if he opposed their attempt to take the stranger.

Namaka had prepared himself for escape by digging in the ground and making a pit under his house, with a tunnel and an opening some distance away.

The warriors from Kalaniopuu surrounded the house, thinking he was inside. They consulted about the best method of killing him, and decided to burn him up. They set fire to the house and destroyed it and went away, believing this stranger had been burned to death.

Namaka easily escaped from Hawaii and crossed over to Maui, where he remained some time, but he found no one whom he wished to take as his lord. Then he went to Oahu, and at last returned to his home on Kauai.

There prophesying about the chiefs of Hawaii, whom he had considered superior to those on Maui and Oahu, but not equal to the royal family of Kauai, he spoke thus: "There is no ruling chief in Hawaii who can step his foot on the tabu sand of Kahamaluihi [Kauai]. There is no war canoe or divine chief who can come to Kauai unless a treaty has been made between the two ruling chiefs."

The natives call this a prophecy of the skilled chief who could fly from Nuuanu Pali, and think it was fulfilled because Kamehameha never conquered Kauai, but secured it by concession from its king.

Note: History repeats itself the world over. Recently the bird-men visited Hawaii and gave exhibitions of flying in aëroplanes. According to old Hawaiian traditions, however, there were bird-men in Hawaii before the white man came, as the foregoing translation from one of the old legends illustrates.

Chapter 18

THE OWLS OF HONOLULU

Pueo

There are three celebrated "owl" localities in the suburbs of Honolulu, one in Manoa Valley, the second near the foot of Punch-bowl Hill, and one at Waikiki.

In Manoa the owl-god lived, and at Waikiki the famous "battle of the owls" was fought.

Manoa Valley is one of the most beautiful rainbow valleys in the world. The highest peaks of the island of Oahu are near the head of the valley. The winds which blow down the Pacific Ocean from the northeast strike these mountain-tops. Each cool breeze leaves its burden of moisture in a fleecy cloud to fall down the mountain-side into the valley. So cloud follows cloud, descending the slopes of the foothills in gentle rain.

Almost all day long the valley is open to the sun, which, looking on the luxuriant verdure and clinging mist, sends its abundant blessing of penetrating light. Rainbows upon rainbows are painted on the steep precipices at the head of the valley. There are arches and double arches of exquisite beauty, smashed fragments of scattered color, broad pillars of glorious fire blazing around green branches of ghost-like trees, great bands of opal hues lying in magnificent masses on the hillside, and lunar rainbows almost circular outlined in soft prismatic shades in the time of the full moon.

When showers creep down the valley one by one, rainbows also chase each other in matchless symmetry of quiet, graceful motion. Sometimes the mist in the doorway of the valley has become so ethereal that splendid arches hang in the apparently clear sky without cloud support.

It is no wonder that from time immemorial the Hawaiians have made the valley the home of royal chiefs, with the rainbow-maiden as their daughter. The story of this child of the skies is told in the legend Ka-hala-o-Puna (The sweet-scented hala-flower of Puna). Woven into this legend is also the legend of the owl-god of the family to which this maiden belonged, for his home as well as hers was in Manoa Valley.

Almost in the middle of the valley is a hill on which many years ago a temple was built and dedicated as the home of the owl-god Pueo. The hill now bears the name "Pu-u" (hill), "Pueo" (owl)—"Puu-pueo," or "The hill of the owl."

It was from this temple that the owl-god rescued the rainbow-maiden three times when she had been thrice killed and buried by her faithless suitor, a chief of Waikiki.

Ka-hala (the hala flower) had followed this chief almost to the lower end of the valley, but she became weary. The angry chief struck her with a bunch of hala nuts, killed her, and buried her under a mass of leaves and dirt near the spot called Aihualama. Pueo, the owl-god, had carefully watched the journey of this one of his people. When he saw her struck down he hastened to the spot swiftly, dashed aside the dirt, pulled out the body, and carried it in his claws back to the head of the valley, where by charms and incantations he healed her wounded head and restored her to life. Soon her beauty came back to her and surrounded her so that she walked as if encompassed with rainbows. Again the Waikiki chief, to whom she had been affianced by her parents, came after her. Again he became angry because she grew weary in the new way by which he led over a high ridge dividing Manoa from a neighboring valley.

A second time he seized a bunch of hala nuts swinging on their long stems, and with this as a club struck her on the head, killing her. He covered the body with ferns and vines and went away. The watching owl-god took the body tenderly, cared for it, and restored it to life. Once more the radiance of a divine chiefess rested in rainbows around the girl and her Manoa Valley home.

The third time the chief called for her she obeyed with trembling, and followed him up the almost precipitous sides of Manoa Valley, over ridges, across valleys and turbulent streams until they came to the ridge by the Waolani Temple in Nuuanu Valley. There he killed her and buried her. But Pueo scratched away the leaves and dirt, and again gave her life.

At the head of Manoa Valley are many waterfalls pouring down the precipices. The longer and most feathery of these falls are said to be the tears of Ka-hala as she suffered from the attacks of the faithless chief of Waikiki.

Pueo, the owl-god, was also Pueo-alii, or "king of owls." He had kahunas (priests) who consulted him by signs, and the aumakuas, or ghost gods, sometimes in oracles. He was thought to be a chief leading his army of ghosts along the hillside below the Puuhonua Temple.*

From his own residence on Owl's Hill he governed all the valley, apparently with much wisdom. It was said that one of the natives in the valley displeased him. He captured the man and at once ordered the death penalty, calling

* This place is now the site of the Castle Home.

him a rebel. The man secured the attention of the owl-god for a moment, and presented the plea that he ought to be permitted to say something for himself before he was punished. This seemed reasonable. The execution was delayed; the man proved that he was innocent of the charge against him. The owl-god established a law that a person must be proved guilty before he could be condemned and punished. This came to be a custom among the Hawaiians as the years passed by.

The legends say that the fairy people, the Menehunes, built a temple and a fort a little farther up the valley above Puu-pueo, at a place called Kukaoo, where even now a spreading hau-tree shelters under its branches the remaining wails and scattered stones of the Kukaoo Temple. It is a very ancient and very noted temple site. Some people say that the owl-god and the fairies became enemies and waged bitter war against each other. At last the owl-god beat the drum of the owl clan and called the owl-gods from Kauai to give him aid.

They flew across the channel in a great cloud and reinforced the owl-god. Then came a fierce struggle between the owls and the little people. The fort and the temple were captured and the Menehunes driven out of the valley.*

* Another legend says that the battle was between the little people and Kualii, a noted chief of Oahu, of comparatively recent date.

KAPOI

The second legendary owl locality is found near the foot of Punchbowl Hill.*

Honolulu as the name of even a village was not known. Apparently there were very few people living along the watercourse coming down Nuuanu Valley. It may have been that even Kou, (the ancient name for Honolulu,) had not been heard. At any rate, the seacoast was a place of growing rushes and nesting birds. A dry heated plain almost entirely destitute of trees extended up to the foothills. Taro patches and little groves of various kinds of trees bordered each watercourse. The population was small and widely scattered. There was a legend of a band of robbers which infested this region. It was almost a "desolate place."

Down Pauoa Valleydashes a stream of beautiful clear water. This passes along the eastern edge of a small extinct crater known as Punchbowl Hill, whose ancient name was Puu-o-waina. The water from this stream was easily diverted into choice taro patch land. Here not far from the upper end of Fort Street at Kahehuna lived a man by the name of Kapoi.

His grass house was decaying. The thatch was falling to pieces. It was becoming a poor shelter

* Head of Fort Street.

from the storms which so frequently swept down the valley. Kapoi went to the Kewalo marsh near the beach, where tall pili grass was growing, to get a bundle of the grass to use for thatching. He found a nest of owl's eggs. He took up his bundle of grass and nest of eggs and returned home.

In the evening he prepared to cook the eggs. With his fire-sticks he had made a fire in his small imu, or oven. An owl flew down and sat on the wall by the gate. Kapoi had almost finished wrapping the eggs in ti leaves and was about to lay them on the hot stones when the owl called to him: "O Kapoi! Give me my eggs."

Kapoi said, "How many eggs belong to you?" The owl replied, "I have seven eggs."

Then Kapoi said, "I am cooking these eggs for I have no fish."

The owl pleaded once more: "O Kapoi! Give me back my eggs."

"But," said Kapoi, "I am already wrapping them for cooking."

Then the owl said: "O Kapoi! You are heartless, and you have no sorrow for me if you do not give back my eggs."

Kapoi was touched, and said, "Come and get your eggs."

Because of this kindness the owl became Kapoi's god, and commanded him to build a heiau (temple) and make a raised place and an altar for sacrifice. The name of the place where he was to build his temple was Manoa. Here he built his temple. He laid a sacrifice and some bananas on the altar, established the day for the tabu to begin and the day also when the tabu should be lifted.

This was talked about by the people. By and by the high chief heard that a man had built a temple for his god, had made it tabu and had lifted the tabu.

Kakuhihewa was living at Waikiki. He was the king after whom the island Oahu was named Oahu-a-Kakuhihewa (The Oahu of Kakuhihewa). This was the especial name of Oahu for centuries. Kakuhihewa encouraged sports and games, and agriculture and fishing. His house was so large that its dimensions have come down in the legends, about 250 x 100 feet. Kakuhihewa was kind, and yet this offence of Kapoi was serious in the eyes of the people in view of their ancient customs and ideas. Kakuhihewa had made a law for his temple which he was building at Waikiki. He had established his tabu over all the people and had made the decree that, if any chief or man should build a temple with a tabu on it and should lift that tabu before the tabu on the king's temple should be over, that chief or man should pay the penalty of death as a rebel.

This king sent out his servants and captured Kapoi. They brought him to Waikiki and placed him in the king's heiau Kapalaha. He was to be killed and offered in sacrifice to the offended god of the king's temple.

KUKAEUNAHIO

The third legendary locality for the owl-gods was the scene of the "battle of the owls." This was at Waikiki. Kapoi was held prisoner in the Waikiki heiau. Usually there was a small, foursquare, stone-walled enclosure in which sacrifices were kept until the time came when they should be killed and placed on the altar. In some such place Kapoi was placed and guarded.

His owl-god was grateful for the return of the eggs and determined to reward him for his kindness and protect him as a worshipper. In some way there must be a rescue. This owl-god was a "family god," belonging only to this man and his immediate household. According to the Hawaiian custom, any individual could select anything he wished as the god for himself and family. Kapoi's owl-god secured the aid of the king of owls, who lived in Manoa Valley on Owl's Hill. The king of owls sent out a call for the owls of all the islands to come and make war against the king of Oahu and his warriors.

Kauai legends say that the sound of the drum of the owl-king was so penetrating that it could be heard across all the channels by the owls on the different islands. In one day the owls of Hawaii, Lanai, Maui and Molokai had gathered at Kalapueo.* The owls of Koolau and Kahikiku, Oahu, gathered together in Kanoniaka-pueo.† The owls of Kauani and Niihau gathered in the place toward the sunset—Pueo-hulu-nui (near Moanalua).

Kakuhihewa had set apart the day of Ka-ne— the day dedicated to the god Ka-ne and given his name—as the day when Kapoi should be sacrificed. This day was the twenty-seventh of the lunar month. In the morning of that day the priests were to slay Kapoi and place him on the altar of the temple in the presence of the king and his warriors.

At daybreak the owls rallied around that temple. As the sun rose, its light was obscured. The owls were clouds covering the heavens. Warriors and chiefs and priests tried to drive the birds away. The owls flew down and tore the eyes and faces of the men of Kakuhihewa. They scratched dirt over them and befouled them.

* A place east of Diamond Head. † A place in Nuuanu Valley.

Such an attack was irresistible—Ka-kuhihewa's men fled, and Kapoi was set free.

Kakuhihewa said to Kapoi: "Your god has mana (miraculous power) greater than my god. Your god is a true god."

Kapoi was saved. The owl was worshipped as a god. The place of that battle was Kukaeunahio-ka-pueo (The-confused-noise-of-owls-rising-in-masses).

Chapter 19

THE TWO FISH FROM TAHITI

Strangers to Hawaiian history should know that to the Hawaiians Tahiti meant any far-away or foreign land. Tahiti belongs to the Society Islands. Centuries ago it was one of the points visited by the Vikings of the Pacific, the Polynesian sea-rovers, among whom certain chiefs of the Hawaiian Islands were not the least noted. They sailed to Tahiti and Samoa and other islands of the great ocean and returned after many months, celebrating their voyages in personal chants.

Thus the names of places many hundreds of miles distant from the Hawaiian group were recorded in the chants and legends of the most famous families of Hawaiian chiefs and kings. Some of the names brought back by the wanderers appear to have been given to places in their own homeland. A large district on the island of Maui, where, it is said, the friends of a Viking would gather for feasting and farewell dancing, was named Kahiki-nui (The great

*Tahiti). A point of land not far from this district was called Keala-i-kahiki (The-way-to-Tahiti). These names are not of recent origin, but are found in the scenes described by roving ancestors noted in genealogies of long ago. Probably about the same time that the Vikings of Scandinavia were roaming along the Atlantic coasts the Pacific seamen were passing from group to group among the Pacific islands.

After many voyages and several years probably the people who never wandered became careless concerning the specific name of the place to which some of their friends had sailed, and included the whole outside world in the comprehensive declaration, "Gone to Tahiti" (Kahiki). At any rate, this has been the usage for some centuries among the Hawaiians.

The story I am about to tell you came to me as a marvellous, mysterious, miraculous myth of the long ago, when strange powers dwelt in both animals and men, and when cannibalism might have been carried on to be reported later under the guise of eating the flesh of beast or fish. In the long ago there were two "fish" crossing the trackless waters of the Pacific Ocean. Their home was in one of the far-away lands, known as Tahiti. These "fish" were great canoes filled with men. They decided that they would like to visit

* "T" and "K" are interchangeable.

some of the lands about which they had heard in the legends related by their fathers.

They knew that certain stars were always in certain places in the sky during a part of every year. By sailing according to these stars at night and the sun by day they felt confident that they could find the wonderful fire-land of Hawaii about which they had been taught in the stories of returned travellers. So the two "fish"—the two boats—after weary days and nights of storm and calm, of soft breeze and strong, continuous winds, found the northeast side of the island of Oahu with its rugged front of steep, precipitous rocks. The travellers landed first on a point of land extending far out into the sea, terminating in a small volcano. Here they made examination of the unfriendly coast and decided to journey entirely around the island, one fish, or boat, going toward the north and the other toward the south. They were apparently intending to pass around the island and find an appropriate location for a settlement. Possibly they planned to make a permanent home or hoped to meet some good community into which they might be absorbed. The point of land which marked the separation of the two companies is called Makapuu. The boat which sailed toward the north found no good resting-place until it came to the fishing-village of Hauula. The stories told by the old natives of the present time do not give any details of the meeting between the strangers and the people residing inthe village. Evidently there was dissension and at last a battle. The whole story is summed up by the Hawaiian legend in the saying: "The fish from Tahiti was caught by the fishermen of Hauula. They killed it and cut it up into pieces for food." Thus the visitors found death instead of friendship, and cannibalism was thereby veiled by calling the victims "fish" and the victory a "catch."

The custom of hiding hints of cannibalistic feasts and more definite human sacrifices under the name of "fish" continued through the centuries even after the discovery of the islands by Captain Cook and the advent of white men. David Malo, a native writer, who, about the year 1840, wrote a concise sketch of Hawaiian history and customs, described the capture of human sacrifices by the priests when needed for temple worship. He says: "The priest conducted a ceremony called Ka-papa-ulua. It was in this way: The priest accompanied by a number of others went out to sea to fish for ulua with hook and line, using squid for bait. If they were unsuccessful and got no ulua they returned to land and went from one house to another, shouting out to the people within and telling them some lie or other and asking them to come outside. If any one did come out, him they killed, and, thrusting a hook in his mouth, carried him away to the heiau [temple]." This sacrifice was called ulua, and was placed before the god of the temple as if it were a fish. Sometimes a part of the body, usually an eye, was eaten during the ceremonies of consecrating the offering to the idol. This custom has passed the test of centuries and probably was the last remnant of cannibalism in the Hawaiian Islands. It endured even to the time of the abolition of the temples and their idols.

The second fish from Tahiti had gone on southward in its journey around the island of Oahu. It passed the rough and desolate craters of Koko Head on the eastern end of the island. It swam by Diamond Head and the beautiful Waikiki Beach. Either the number of the inhabitants was so large that they were afraid to make any stay or else they preferred to make the complete circuit of the island before locating, for they evidently made only a very short stay wherever they landed, and then hurried on their journey. By the time they reached Kaena, the northwestern cape of Oahu, they were evidently anxious concerning their missing companions. Not a boat on the miles of water between Kaena and Kahuku, the most northerly point on the island. The legend says that the fish changed itself into a man and went inland to search the coast for its friend, but the search was unsuccessful. It was now a weary journey from point to point, watching the sea and exploring all the spots on the beach where it seemed as if there was any prospect of finding a trace of their expected friends. Where a break in the coral reef permitted their boat to approach the land they forced their way to shore. Then when the thorough search failed again, the boat was pushed out over the line of white inrolling breakers to the great sea until at last the Tahitians came to Kahuku.

Now they appeared no longer as "fish," but went to the village at Kahuku as men. They made themselves at home among the people and were invited to a great feast. They heard the story of a battle with a great fish at Hauula and the capture of the monster. They heard how it had been cut up and its fragments widely distributed among the villages on the northwest coast. Evidently provision had been made for several great feasts. The people of Kahuku, although several miles distant from Hauula, had received their portion. The friendly strangers must share this great gift with them. But the men from Tahiti with heavy hearts recognized the fragments as a part of their companion. They could not partake of the feast, but by kindliness and strategy they managed not only to decline the invitation, but also to secure some portions of the flesh to carry down to the sea. These were thrown into the water, and immediately came to life. They had the color of blood as a reminder of the death from which they had been reclaimed. Ever after they bore the name "Hilu-ula," or "the red Hilu."

Then the "fish" from Tahiti went on around to Hauula. They went up to the tabu land back of Hauula. They pulled up the tabu flags. Then they dammed up the waters of the valley above the village until there was sufficient for a mighty flood. The storms from the heavy clouds drove the people into their homes. Then the Tahitians opened the flood-gates of their mountain reservoir and let the irresistible waters down upon the village. The houses and their inhabitants were swept into the sea and destroyed. Thus vengeance came upon the cannibals.

The Tahitians were "fish," therefore they went back into the ocean to swim around the islands. Sometimes they came near enough to the haunts of fishermen to be taken for food. They bear the name "hilu." But there are two varieties. The red hilu is cooked and eaten, but never eaten without having felt the power of fire. The trace of the cannibal feast is always over its flesh. Therefore it has to be removed by purification of the flames over which it is prepared for food. The blue hilu, the natives say, is salted and eaten uncooked. Thus the legend says the two fish came from Tahiti, and thus they became the origin of some of the beautiful fish whose colors flash like the rainbow through the clear waters of Hawaii.

Another legend somewhat similar to this is told by the natives of Hauula. There is a valley near this village called Kaipapau (The-valley-of-the-shallow-sea). Here lived an old kahuna, or priest, who always worshipped the two great gods Ka-ne and Kanaloa. These gods had their home in the place where the old man continually worshipped them, but they loved to go away from time to time for a trip around the island. Once the gods came to their sister's home and received from her dried fish for food. This they carried to the sea and threw into the waters, where it became alive again and swam along the coast while the gods journeyed inland. By and by they came to the little river on which the old man had his home. The gods went inland along the bank of the river, and the fish turned also, forcing their way over the sand-bank which marked the mouth of the little stream. Then they went up the river to a pool before the place where the gods had stopped. Ever since, when high water has made the river accessible, these fish, named ulua, have come to the place where the gods were worshipped by the kahuna and where they rested and drank awa with him. When the gods had taken enough of the awa of the priest they turned away with the warning that when he heard a great noise on the shore he must not go down to see what the people were doing, but ask what the excitement was about, and if it was a shark or a great fish he was to remain at home. He must not go to that place.

A few days later a big wave came up from the sea and swept over the beach. When the water flowed back there was left a great whale, the tail on the shore and the head out in the sea. The people came to see the whale. They thought that it was dead. They played on its back and leaped into the deep waters from its head. Their shouts of joy and loud laughter reached the ears of the priest, who was living inland. Then the people came to the riverside to gather vines and flowers with which to make wreaths. Probably it was the intention of the villagers to cut the great fish into pieces and have a feast. The old priest was very anxious to see the marvellous fish. He forgot the warning of the gods and went to the seaside. The people shouted for the old man to come quickly. The old priest stood by the tail of the great fish. As if to welcome him the tail moved. He climbed on the back and ran to the head and leaped into the sea. The people cheered the priest as he returned to the beach and a second time approached the whale. Again there was the motion of the tail, and again the priest ran along the back, but as he leaped the whale caught him and carried him away to Tahiti. Therefore a name was given to a point of land not far from this place—the name "Ka-loe-o-ka-palaoa" (The cape of the whale).

Chapter 20

IWA, THE NOTABLE THIEF OF OAHU

In ancient Hawaii thieving was an honorable profession. It required cultivation as well as natural ability. Even as late as the days of Captain Cook and his discovery of the Hawaiian Islands there is the record of a chief whose business was to steal successfully. When Captain Cook discovered the island Kauai, a chief by the name of Kapu-puu (The-tabu-hill) was one of the first to go out to the ships. He went saying, "There is plenty of iron [hao]. I will 'hao' [steal] the 'hao,' for to 'hao' [to plunder] is my livelihood "—as one historian expressed the saying: "To plunder is with me house and land." The chief, however, was detected in the act and was shot and killed. The natives never seemed to blame Captain Cook for the death of that chief. The thief was unsuccessful. Really, the sin of stealing consisted in being detected.

The story of Iwa, the successful thief, is back in the days when Umi was king of Hawaii, four-

teen generations of kings before Kamehameha
the First. The king Umi was well known in
Hawaiian historical legends, and many important events are dated with his reign as the refer-
ence-point.

In Puna, Hawaii, while Umi was king, there
lived a fisherman by the name of Keaau. He was
widely known for his skill in fishing with a wonderful shell It was one of the leho shells, and
was used in catching squid. Its name was Kalo-
kuna. Keaau always returned from fishing with
his canoe full. After a time he was talked about
all around the island, and Umi heard about the
magic leho of the fisherman.

At that time Umi dwelt in Kona, where he
was fishing after the custom of those days. He
sent a messenger commanding the fisherman to
bring his shell to Kona, where he could show its
power and his skill. Then the king, who had the
right to take all the property of any of his subjects, took the shell from the fisherman.

Keaau's heart became very sore for the loss of
his shell, so he went to a man on Hawaii who was
skilled in theft and asked him to secretly steal
the leho and return it to him. He brought his
canoe filled with his property—a pig, some fruit
and awa and the black-and-white and spotted
tapa sheets—to give to the thief who could get
back his shell. But neither this thief nor any oth-

ers on the islands of Hawaii, Maui or Molokai was sufficiently skilful to give him any aid.

Then he passed on to Oahu, where he met a man fishing, who, according to the custom of the people, invited him to land and accept hospitality. When the feast was over, they asked him the object of his journey. He told the story of the loss of his leho, and said that he was travelling to find "a thief able to steal back the shell taken by the strong hand of the chief of Hawaii."

Then the Oahu people told him about Iwa and his marvellous skill in plundering. They directed him to row his canoe around by Makapo and then land, and he would find a boy without a malo (loin cloth). He must give him the offering—the good things brought in the canoe. He found the boy and placed before him the gifts. They killed the pig and cooked it over hot stones. Then they had a feast, and the boy-thief asked the traveller why he had come to him. The fisherman told all his trouble and asked Iwa to go with him to recover the shell. To this Iwa consented, and after a night's rest prepared to go to Hawaii.

When the time came for the journey he placed Keaau in front and took his place to steer and paddle. The name of his paddle was Kapahi, which means "Scatter the water." Iwa told the fisherman to look sharp at the land before them; then he talked to his paddle, saying, "Let the ocean meet the sea of Iwa." He struck his paddle once into the sea and the canoe rushed by the little islands along the coast and passed to Niihau. From Niihau in four paddle-strokes the canoe lay before the coast of Hawaii, where Umi and his chiefs were fishing. One of the canoes had a palm-branch house built over it to shade the fisherman. Iwa asked if that was the royal canoe, and, learning that it was, quickly backed his canoe around a headland and prepared to dive, saying to his friend, "I will go and steal that leho."

He leaped into the water and sank to the bottom of the ocean. He walked along under the sea aided by his magic power until he came to the place where the king's canoes were floating. Over the side of the king's boat hung the cord to which the shell was fastened. Iwa rose quietly under the canoe and caught the leho, slowly drew it down to the bottom, broke the cord and fastened it to sharp rocks, and then went back to the place where Keaau was waiting for him. All along the way giant squid and devilfish fought him and tried to take the shell from his hands, but by incantations and the power of his gods he escaped to the canoe, and, leaping in, gave the leho to the fisherman, and paddled away to Puna. There he dwelt with Keaau for a little while.

When the boy-thief took the cord of Umi he
thought that a very great squid had seized the
shell, and let the line run, afraid lest it might
break and the shell be lost, but when he tried to
pull he found it fast below. He sent to the land
for all the people who could dive, but none of
them could go to the bottom. Ten days and ten
nights he waited in his canoe. Then he sent over
all the island Hawaii for those who knew how to
dive in deep water, but all the noted divers
failed. The messenger came to the place where
Iwa was staying. Keaau was away fishing. Iwa
took the messenger to the place where the fisherman dried squid and showed him a great
many already caught. Then Iwa said, "Go back
and tell your king that the leho is not on the
line, but a rock is holding it fast."

The messenger returned to the king and
reported the saying of Iwa. Then the king sent
swift men to run and bring Iwa to him. The boy
agreed to go to Umi, and sped more swiftly than
the runners sent for him. When he stood before
Umi he told the king all his story and leaped
into the sea, diving down, breaking the rock and
bringing up the piece to which the line had
been tied. Umi then wanted Iwa to return to
Puna and steal that leho for him. Iwa went back
to the fisherman's house, and that night stole
the shell for the king.

When Umi received the shell he rejoiced greatly at the skill of this thief. Then he thought about his tabu stone axe in Waipio Valley, and wished to test this boy-thief again.

This sacred stone axe really belonged to Umi, the son of Liloa, but it had been kept in the tabu heiau (sacred temple) of Pakaalana, in Waipio Valley. Two old women were guardians of this tabu axe. It was tied fast in the middle of a line. One end of that cord was fastened around the neck of one old woman, and one end around the neck of the other. Thus they wore the cord as a lei (wreath) of that sacred stone axe of Umi. When Umi asked the thief if he would steal this axe, Iwa said he would try, but he waited until the sun was almost down, then he ran swiftly to Waipio Valley as if he were a messenger of the king, calling to the people and establishing a tabu over the land:

"Sleep—sleep for the sacred stone axe of Umi.
Tabu—let no man go forth from his house.
Tabu—let no dog bark.
Tabu—let no rooster crow.
Tabu—let no pig make a noise.
Sleep—sleep till the tabu is raised."

Five times he called the tabu, beginning at Puukapu near Waimea, as he went to the guarded path to Waipio. When he had established this tabu he travelled down to the place where the old women guarded the axe. He called again, "Has sleep come to you two?" And they answered, "Here we are; we are not asleep." He called again: "Where are you? I would touch that sacred axe of Umi and return and report that this hand has held the sacred stone axe of the king."

He came near and took the axe and pulled the ends of the string tight around the necks of the old women, choking them and throwing them over. Then he broke the string and ran swiftly up the path over the precipice. The old women disentangled themselves and began to cry out, "Stolen is the tabu axe of Umi, and the thief has gone up toward Waimea." The people followed Iwa from place to place, but could not overtake him, and soon lost him.

Iwa went on to the king's place and lay down to sleep. As morning drew near the king's people found him asleep and told the king he had not been away, but when Iwa was awake he was called to the king, who said, "Here, you have not got the tabu stone axe."

"Perhaps not," said the boy, "but here is an axe which I found last night. Will you look at it?" The king saw that it was his tabu axe, and wondered at the magic power of the thief, for he thought it impossible to go to Waipio and return in the one night, and he knew how difficult it would be to get the axe and escape from the people.

He determined to give Iwa another trial—a contest with the best thieves of his kingdom. He asked if Iwa would consent to a death contest. The one surpassing in theft should receive reward. The defeated should be put to death. This plan seemed right to the thief from Oahu. It would be a great battle—one against six.

The king called his clan of six thieves and Iwa, and told them that he would set apart two houses in which they could put their plunder. That night they were to go out and steal, and the one whose house contained the most property should be the victor. The report of the contest spread all through the village, and the people prepared to hide their property.

Iwa lay down to sleep while the six men quietly and swiftly passed among the people, stealing whatever they could. When they saw Iwa asleep they pitied him for his certain death. Toward morning their house was almost full, and still Iwa slept. The six thieves were very tired and hungry, so they prepared a feast and awa. They ate and drank until overcome with drunkenness. A little before dawn they also fell asleep.

Iwa arose, hastened to the house failed by the six thieves, and hastily removed all their plunder to his own house. Then he went quietly to Umi's sleeping-house, and, showing his great skill, removed the tapa sheets from the bed in which the king was sleeping, and piled them on the other things in his house. Then he lay down again as if asleep.

The morning cold fell on the king, and he was chilled, and awoke, feeling for the sheets, but could not find them. He remembered the contest, and as the daylight rested upon them he called the people together.

They went to the house of the six thieves and opened it to look for their plunder, and not one thing was there. It was entirely empty. After this they went to Iwa's house. When the door was open they saw the king's tapa sheets on all the other plunder. The six thieves were put to death, and Iwa was honored for some years as the very dear friend of the king and the most adroit thief in the kingdom.

After a time he longed for the place of his birth, and he asked Umi to send him back to his parents. Umi filled a double canoe with good things and let him go back to the green-sided pali (or precipice) of the district of Koolau, on the island Oahu.

Chapter 21

PIKOI THE RAT-KILLER

Long, long ago in the Hawaiian Islands, part of the children of a chief's family might be born real boys and girls, while others would be "gods" in the form of some one of the various kinds of animals known to the Hawaiians. These "gods" in the family could appear as human beings or as animals. They were guardians of the family, or, perhaps it should be said, they watched carefully over some especial brother or sister, doing all sorts of marvellous things such as witches and fairies like to do for those whom they love.

In a family on Kauai six girl-gods were born and only one real gift and one real boy. These "gods" were all rats and were named "Kikoo," which was the name of the bow used with an arrow for rat-shooting. They were "Bow-of-the-heaven," "Bow-of-the-earth," "Bow-of-the-mountain," "Bow-of-the-ocean," "Bow-of-the-night" and "Bow-of-the-day."

These rat-sister-gods seemed to have charge of their brother and his sports. His incantations and chants were made in their names. The real sister was named "Ka-ui-o-Manoa" ("The Beauty of Manoa"). She was a very beautiful woman, who came to Oahu to meet Pawaa, the chief of Manoa Valley, and marry him. He was an aikane (bosom friend) to Kakuhihewa, the king of Oahu. They made their home at Kahaloa in Manoa Valley. They also had Kahoiwai in the upper end of the valley.

The boy's name was Pikoi-a-ka-Alala (Pikoi, the son of Alala). In his time the chief sport seemed to be hunting rats with bows and arrows. Pikoi as a child became very skilful. He was very clear and far sighted, and surpassed all the men of Kauai in his ability to kill hidden and far-off rats. The legends say this was great-ly due to the aid given by his rat-sisters. At that same time there was on Kauai a very wonderful dog, Puapualenalena (Pupua, the yellow). That dog was very intelligent and very swift.

One day it ran into the deep forest and saw a small boy who was successfully shooting rats. The dog joined him. The dog caught ten rats while Pikoi shot ten.

Some days later the two friends went into a wilderness. In that day's contest the dog caught forty and the boy shot forty. Again and again they tried, but the boy could not win from the dog, nor could the dog beat the boy.

After a while they became noted throughout Kauai. The story of the skill of Pikoi was related on Oahu and repeated even on Hawaii. His name was widely known, although few had seen him.

One day his father Alala told Pikoi that he wanted to see his daughter in Manoa Valley. They launched their canoe and sailed across the channel, leaving the marvellous dog behind.

Midway in the channel Pikoi cried out: "Look! There is a great squid!" It was the squid Kaka-hee, who was a god. Pikoi took his bow and fitted an arrow to it, for he saw the huge creature hiding in a pit deep in the coral. The squid rose up from its cave and followed the boat, stretching out its long arms and trying to seize them. The boy shot the monster, using the bow and arrow belonging to the ocean. The enemy died in a very little while. This was near the cape of Kaena. The name of the land at that place is Kakahee. These monsters of the ocean were called Kupuas. It was believed that they were evil gods, always hoping to inflict some injury on man.

Pikoi and his father landed and went up to Manoa Valley. There they met Ka-ui-o-Manoa and wept from great joy as they embraced each other. A feast was prepared, and all rested for a time.

Pikoi wandered away down the valley and out toward the lands overlooking the harbor of Kou (Honolulu). On the plain called Kula-o-ka-hua he saw a chiefess with some of her people. This plain was the comparatively level ground below Makiki Valley. Apparently it was covered at that time with a small shrub, or dwarf-like tree, called aweoweo. Rats were hiding under the shelter of the thick leaves and branches.

Pikoi went to the place where the people were gathered. The chiefess was Kahamaluihi, the wife of the king Kakuhihewa. With her was her famous arrow-shooting chiefess, Ke-pana-kahu, who was shooting against Mainele, the noted rat-shooting chief of her husband. The queen had been betting with Mainele and had lost because he was a better shot that day than her friend. She was standing inside tabu lines under a shaded place, but Pikoi went in and stood by her. She was angry for a moment, and asked why he was there. He made a pleasant answer about wishing to see the sport.

She asked if he could shoot. He replied that he had been taught a little of the art, so she offered him the use of a bow and arrow and at that he said, "This arrow and this bow are not good for this kind of shooting."

She laughed at him. "You are only a boy; what can you know about rat-hunting?"

He was a little nettled, and broke the bow and arrow, saying, "These things are of no use whatever."

The chiefess was really angry, and cried out, "What do you mean by breaking my things, you deceitful child?"

Meanwhile Pikoi's father had missed him and had learned from his daughter that the high chiefess was having a rat-shooting contest. He took Pikoi's bows and arrows wrapped in tapa and went down with the bundle on his back.

Pikoi took a bow and arrow from the bundle and persuaded the high chiefess to make a new wager with Mainele. The queen, in kindly mood, placed treasure against treasure.

Mainele prepared to shoot first, agreeing with Pikoi to make fifteen the number of shots for the first trial.

Pikoi pointed out rat after rat among the shrubs until Mainele had killed fourteen. Then the boy cried: "There is only one shot more. Shoot that rat whose whiskers are by a leaf of that aweoweo tree. The body is concealed, but I can see the whiskers. Shoot that rat, O Mainele!"

Mainele looked the shrubs all over carefully, but could not see the least sign of a rat. The people went near and thrust arrows among the leaves, but could see nothing.

Then Mainele said: "There is no rat in that place. I have looked where you said. You are a lying child when you say that you see the whiskers of a rat."

Pikoi insisted that the rat was there. Mainele was vexed, and said: "Behold all the treasure I have won from the chiefess and the treasure which we are now betting. You shall have it all if you shoot and strike the whiskers of any rat in that small tree. If you do not strike a rat I will simply claim the present bet."

Then Pikoi took out of the bundle held by his father a bow and an arrow. He carefully strung his bow and fixed the arrow, pointing the eye of that arrow toward the place pointed out before.

The queen said, "That is a splendid bow." Her caretaker, however, was watching the beautiful eyes of the boy, and his general appearance.

Pikoi was softly chanting to himself. This was his incantation or prayer to his sister-gods:

"There he is, there he is, O Pikoi!
  Alala is the father,
  Koukou is the mother.
  The divine sisters were born.
  O Bent-bow-of-heaven!
  O Bent-bow-of-earth!
  O Bent-bow-of-the-mountain!
  O Bent-bow-of-the-ocean!

O Bent-bow-of-the-night!
O Bent-bow-of-the-day!
  O Wonderful Ones!
  O Silent Ones!
     Silent.
There is that rat—
That rat in the leaves of the aweoweo,
By the fruit of the aweoweo,
By the trunk of the aweoweo.
Large eyes have you, O Mainele;
But you did not see that rat.
If you had shot, O Mainele,
You would have hit the whiskers of that rat—
You would have had two rats—two.
Another comes—three rats—three!"

Then Mainele said: "You are a lying child. I, Mainele, am a skilful shooter. I have struck my rat in the mouth or the foot or any part of the body, but no one has ever pierced the whiskers. You are trying to deceive."

Pikoi raised his bow, felt his arrow, and said to his father, "What arrow is this?"

His father replied, "That is the arrow Mahu, which eats the flower of the lehua-tree."

Pikoi said: "This will not do. Hand me another." Then his father gave him Lau-kona (The-arrow-which- strikes-the-strong-leaf), but the boy said: "This arrow has killed only sixty rats and its eye is smooth. Give me one more."

His father handed him the Huhui (The-bunched-together), an arrow having three or four sharp notches in the point.

Pikoi took it, saying, "This arrow wins the treasure," and went toward the tree, secretly repeating his chant.

Then he let the arrow go twisting and whirling around, striking and entangling the whiskers of three rats.

Mainele saw this wonderful shooting, and delivered all the treasures he had wagered. But Pikoi said he had not really won until he had killed fourteen more rats, so he shot again a very long arrow among the thick leaves of the shrubs, and the arrow was full of rats strung on it from end to end hanging on it by forties.

The people stood with open mouths in silent astonishment, and then broke out in wildest enthusiasm.

While they were excited the boy and his father secretly went away to their home in Manoa Valley and remained there with Ka-ui-o-Manoa a long time, not visiting Waikiki or the noted places of the island Oahu.

Kakuhihewa, the king, heard about this strange contest and tried to find the wonderful boy. But he had entirely disappeared. The caretaker of the high chiefess was the only one who had carefully observed his eyes and his general appearance, but she had no knowledge of his home or how he had disappeared.

She suggested that all the men of Oahu be called, district by district, to bring offerings to the king, two months being allowed each district, lest there should be a surplus of gifts and the people impoverished and reduced to a state of famine.

Five years passed. In the sixth year the Valley of Manoa was called upon to bring its gifts.

Pikoi had grown into manhood and had changed very much in his general appearance. His hair was very long, failing far down his body. He asked his sister to cut his hair, and persuaded her to take her husband's shark-tooth knives. She refused at first, saying, "These knives are tabu because they belong to the chief." At last she took the teeth—one above, or outside of the hair, and one inside—and tried to cut the hair, but it was so thick and stout that the handles broke, and she gave up, saying, "Your hair is the hair of a god." However, that night while he slept his rat-sister-gods came and gnawed off his hair, some eating one place and some another. It was not even. From this the ancient saying arose: "Look at his hair. It was cut by rats."

Pawaa, the chief, came home and found his wife greatly troubled. She told him all that she had done, and he said: "Broken were the handles, not the teeth of the shark. If the teeth had broken, that would have been bad."

Pikoi's face had been discolored by the sister-gods, so that when he appeared with ragged hair no one knew him—not even his father and sister. He put on some beautiful garlands of lehua flowers and went with the Manoa people to Waikiki to appear before the king.

The people were feasting, surf-riding and enjoying all kinds of sports before they should be called to make obeisance to their king.

Pikoi wandered down to the beach at Ulu-kou* where the queen and her retinue were surfriding. While he stood near the water the queen came in on a great wave which brought her before him. He asked for her papa (surf-board) but she said it was tabu to any one but herself. Any other taking that surf-board would be killed by the servants.

Then the chiefess, who was with the queen when Pikoi shot the rats of Makiki, came to the shore. The queen said, "Here is a surf-board you can use." The chiefess gave him her board and did not know him. He went out into the sea at Waikiki where the people were sporting. The surf was good only in one place, and that was tabu to the queen. So Pikoi allowed a wave to carry him across to the high combers upon which she was riding. She waited for him, because she

* Near the present Moana Hotel.

was pleased with his great beauty, although he had tried to disguise himself.

She asked him for one of his beautiful leis of lehua flowers, but he said he must refuse because she was tabu. "No! No!" she replied. "Nothing is tabu for me to receive. It will be tabu after I have worn it." So he gave her the garland of flowers. That part of the surf is named Kalehua-wike (The-loosened-lehua).

Then he asked her to launch her board on the first wave and let him come in on the second. She did not go, but caught the second wave as he swept by. He saw her, and tried to cut across from his wave to the next. She followed him, and very skilfully caught that wave and swept to the beach with him.

A great cry came from the people. "That boy has broken the tabu!" "There is death for the boy!"

The king, Kakuhihewa, heard the shout and looked toward the sea. He saw the tabu queen and that boy on the same surf-wave.

He called to his officers: "Go quickly and seize that young chief who has broken the tabu of the queen. He shall not live."

The officers ran to him, seized him, tossed him around, tore off his malo, struck him with clubs, and began to kill him.

Pikoi cried: "Stop! Wait until I have had word with the king."

They led him to the place where the king waited. Some of the people insulted him, and threw dirt and stones upon him as he passed.

The king was in kindly mood and listened to his explanation instead of ordering him to be killed at once.

While he was speaking before the king, the queen and the other women came. One of them looked carefully at him and recognized some peculiar marks on his side. She exclaimed, "There is the wonderful child who won the victory from Mainele. He is the skilful rat-shooter."

The king said to the woman, "You see that this is a fine-looking young man, and you are trying to save him."

The woman was vexed, and insisted that this was truly the rat-shooter.

Then the king said: "Perhaps we should try him against Mainele. They may shoot here in this house." This was the house called the Hale-noa (Free-for-all-the-family). The king gave the law of the contest. "You may each shoot like the arrows on your hands [the ten fingers] and five more—fifteen in all."

Pikoi was afraid of this contest. Mainele had his own weapons, while Pikoi had nothing, but he looked around and saw his father, Alala, who now knew him. The father had the tapa bundle of bows and arrows. The woman recognized him, and called, "Behold the man who has the bow and arrow for this boy."

Pikoi told Mainele to shoot at some rats under the doorway. He pointed them out one after the other until twelve had been killed.

Pikoi said: "There is one more. His body cannot be seen, but his whiskers are by the edge of the stone step."

Mainele denied that any rat was there, and refused to shoot.

The king commanded Pikoi not to shoot at any rat under the door, but to kill real rats, as Mainele had done.

Pikoi took his bow, bent it, and drew it out until it stretched from one side of the house to the other. The arrow was very long. He called to his opponent to point out rats.

Mainele could not point out any. Nor could the king see one around the house.

Pikoi shot an arrow at the doorstep and killed a rat which had been hiding underneath.

Then Pikoi shot a bent-over, old-man rat in one corner; then pointed to the ridge-pole and chanted his usual chant, ending this time:

> "Straight the arrow strikes
>   Hitting the mouth of the rat,
>   From the eye of the arrow to the end
>   Four hundred—four hundred!"

The king said: "Shoot your 'four hundred—
four hundred.' Mainele shall pick them up, but if
the eye of your arrow fails to find rats, you die."

Pikoi shot his arrow, which glanced along the
ridge-pole under the thatch, striking rat after
rat until the arrow was full from end to end,—
hundreds and hundreds.

The high chief Pawaa knew his brother-in-
law, embraced him, and wailed over his trouble.
Then, grasping his war-club, he stepped out of
the house to find the men who had struck Pikoi
and torn off his malo. He struck them one after
the other on the back of the neck, killing twenty men. The king asked his friend why he had
done this. Pawaa replied, "Because they evilly
handled my brother-in-law,—the only brother
of my wife, 'The Beauty of Manoa.'"

The king said, "That is right."

The people who had insulted Pikoi and
thrown dirt upon him began to run away and
try to hide. They fled in different directions.

Pikoi caught his bow and fixed an arrow and
again chanted to his rat-sister-gods, ending with
an incantation against those who were in flight:

"Strike! Behold there are the rats—the men!
    The small man,
    The large man,
    The tall man,

The short man,
The panting coward.
Fly, arrow! and strike!
    Return at last!"

The arrow pierced one of the fleeing men, leaped aside to strike another, passed from side to side around those who had pitied him, striking only those who had been at fault, searching out men as if it had eyes, at last returning to its place in the tapa bundle. The arrow was given the name Ka-pua-akamai-loa (The-very-wise-arrow). Very many were punished by this wise arrow.

Wondering and confused was the great assemblage of chiefs, and they said to each other, "We have no warrior who can stand before this very skilful young man."

The king gave Pikoi an honorable place among his chiefs, making him his personal great rat-hunter. The queen adopted him as her own child.

No one had heard Pikoi's name during all these wonderful experiences. When he chanted his prayer in which he gave his name, he had sung so softly that no one could hear what he was saying. Therefore the people called him Ka-pana-kahu-ahi (The-fire-building-shooter), because his arrow was like fire in its destruction.

Pikoi returned to Manoa Valley with Pawaa and his father and sister. There he dwelt for some time in a great grass house, the gift of the king.

Kakuhihewa planned to give him his daughter in marriage, but opportunity for new experiences in Hawaii came to Pikoi, and he went to that island, where he became a noted bird-shooter as well as a rat-hunter, and had his final contest with Mainele.

Mainele was very much ashamed when the king commanded him to gather up not only the dead bodies of all the people who were slain by that very wise arrow, but the bodies of the rats also. He was compelled to make the ground clean from the blood of the dead. He ran away and hid himself in a village with people of the low class until an opportunity came to go to the island Hawaii to attempt a new record for himself with his bow and arrow.

Chapter 22

KAWELO

Many Kawelos are named in the legends of the islands of Oahu and Kauai, but one only was the strong, the mighty warrior who destroyed a gigantic enemy who used trees for spears. He was known as Kawelo-lei-makua when mentioned in the genealogies.

Kawelo's great-uncle, Kawelo-mahamahaia, was the king of Kauai. The land prospered and was quiet under him. When he died, the people worshipped him as a god. They said he had become a divine shark, watching over the seacoasts of his island. At last they thought it had become a stone god—one point the head and one the tail, one side red and the other black. His grandson, Kawelo-aikanaka, who became king of Kauai, was born the same day that brought Kawelo-lei-makua into the world. They were always known as Aikanaka and Kawelo. There was also born that same day Kauahoa, who became the giant of Kauai, and the person-

173

al enemy of Kawelo. In their infancy the three boys were taken by their grandparents to Wailua, and brought up near each other under different caretakers.

Some of the legends say that Kawelo's oldest brother, Kawelo-mai-huna, was born an eepa—a child poorly formed, but having miraculous powers. When born, the servants wrapped this child in a tapa sheet and thought to bury it, but a fierce storm arose. There were sharp lightnings and loud thunder. Strong winds swept around the house. So they put the bundle in a small calabash, covered it with a feather cloak, and hung it in the top of the house. The grandparents came and prophesied a marvellous future for this child. The father started to take down the calabash, but saw only a cloud of red feathers whirling and concealing all the upper corner. The old people, with heads bowed down, were uttering incantations. There came a sound of raindrops falling on the leaves of the forest trees, and a rainbow stood over the door. The voices of beautiful green birds (the Elepaio) were heard all around, and rats ran over the thatch of the roof. Then the old people said: "This child has become an eepa. He will appear as man or bird or fish or rat."

Other children were born, then Kawelo, and last of all his faithful younger brother, Kama-

lama. The old people who took care of Kawelo
were his grandparents. They taught the signs and
incantations and magic of Hawaiian thought.
They frequently went inland to the place where
their best food was growing. They always prepared large calabashes full of poi and other food,
thinking to have plenty when they returned; but
each time all the food was eaten. They decided
that it was better to provide sports for Kawelo
than to leave him idle while they were away, so
they went to the forest with their servants and
made a canoe. After many days their work was
done, and they returned to prepare food. Poi was
made, and all kinds of food were placed in the
ovens for cooking. Then they heard a sound like
that of a strong wind tearing through the forest.
They heard the squeaking voices of many rats.
Soon they went to see the canoe in the forest, but
it was gone. They returned home to eat the poi
and cooked food, but they were all gone—only
the leaves in which the food had been wrapped
lay in the oven. Kawelo told his grandparents
that little people with rat-whiskers had carried
the boat down to the river and then had eaten all
the food. One, larger than the others, had called
to him, "E Kawelo, here is your plaything, the
canoe."

Kawelo went down to the river. All day long
he paddled up and down the river, and all day

long his strength grew with each paddle-stroke. Thus day by day he paddled from morning until night, and no one in all the island had such renown for handling a canoe.

The other boys were carefully trained in all games of skill, in boxing, wrestling, spear-throwing, back-breaking, and other athletic exercises. Kauahoa was very jealous of Kawelo's plaything, and asked his caretakers to make something for him, so they made a kite (a pe-a) and gave it to their foster-child. That kite rose far up in the heavens. Loud were the shouts of the people as they saw this beautiful thing in the sky. Kawelo asked for a kite, and in a few days took one out to fly by the side of Kauahoa's kite. He let out the string and it rose higher and higher, and the people cheered loudly. Kawelo came nearer and nearer to Kauahoa and pulled his kite down slowly and then let it go quickly. His kite leaped from side to side, and twisted its strings around that held by Kauahoa and broke it, and the kite was blown far over the forest, at a place called Kahoo leina a pe-a (The-kite-falling). Kawelo said the wind was to blame, so Kauahoa, although very angry, could find no cause for fighting. Then the grandparents taught Kawelo to box and wrestle and handle the war spear. Thus the boys grew in stature and in enmity.

After a time the king of Kauai died and Aikanaka became king. The legends say the rats warned Kawelo, and he and his grandparents fled to the island of Oahu. The boat flew over the sea like a malolo (flying-fish), leaping over the waves at the strong stroke of Kawelo. The rats under their king were concealed in the canoe, and were carried over to the new home. Kawelo's elder brothers and parents had been living for some time on the beach of Waikiki near Ulukou* by the mouth of the stream Apuakehau. The grandparents took Kawelo and Kamalama inland and found a beautiful place among taro patches and cultivated fields for their home. It was said that when they came to the beach one young man went down into the water and carried the canoe inland. Kawelo called him and adopted him as one of the family. The boy's name was Kalaumeke (A-kind-of-ti-leaf). The boy said he was not as strong as he appeared to be, for he had the aid of many little long-whiskered people; his real power lay in spear-throwing and club-fighting. There was only one other young man who was his equal —a youth from Ewa, whose name was Kaeleha. Kawelo sent for this man and took him into his family. They dwelt for some time, cultivating the place where the royal lands now lie, back of the Waikiki beach.

* Site of Moana Hotel.

One day they heard great shouting and clapping of hands on the beach, and Kawelo went down to see the sport. His brothers had been well taught all the arts of boxing and wrestling, and they were very strong; but they were not able to overthrow a very strong man from Halemanu. Kawelo challenged the strong man. His elder brothers ridiculed him, but Kawelo persevered. The strong man was much larger and taller than Kawelo. He uttered his boast as Kawelo came before him. "Strong is the koa* of Halemanu. The kona [wind] cannot bend it." Kawelo boasted in reply, "Mauna Waialeale will try against Mauna Kaala." Then the strong man said: "When I call 'swing your hands' we will fall against each other." With this word he advanced and struck at Kawelo, bending him over, but not knocking him down. Kawelo returned the blow with such force that the mighty boxer fell dead. Kawelo gave the body to the king of Oahu to be carried as a sacrifice to the gods in the heiau, or temple, Lualualei at Waianae. "This is said to have been a very ancient temple belonging to the chief Kakuhihewa."

Kawelo's brothers were greatly mortified to see their younger brother accomplish what they had failed to do, so in their shame they returned to Kauai with their parents.

* A tree—Acacia koa.

The king of Oahu gave Kawelo lands. His grandparents built him a house. It was well thatched except the top. He was a high tabu chief, and the kahunas (priests) said he must finish it with the work of his own hands. This he thought he would do with the beautiful feathers of the red and yellow birds. He lay down and slept. When he awoke he saw his rat-brother, who had miraculous power, finishing all the roof with most beautiful feathers of red and gold. The king of Oahu came to see this wonderful place, and blessed it, and lifted his tabu from it so that it would belong fully to Kawelo, although it was more beautiful than that of the king himself.

Kawelo learned the hula (dance), and went around the island attending all hula gatherings until the people called him "the great hula chief." At the village of Kaneohe he met the most beautiful woman of that part of the island, Kane-wahine-ike-aoha. He married her, gave up the hula, and returned home to learn the art of battle with spears and clubs. No one was more strong or more skilful than his wife's father. Kawelo sent his wife to the other side of the island to ask her father to teach him to fight with the war-club. She went to her father and persuaded him to aid Kawelo. For many days they practised together, until Kawelo was mighty in handling both spear and club.

After this Kawelo learned the prayers and incantations and offerings upon which good fishing depended. Then he took the fisherman and went out in the ocean to do battle with a great fish which had terrified the people of Oahu many years. This was a kupua, or magic fish, possessing exceeding great powers. As they went out from Waikiki, with one stroke of the paddle Kawelo sent the canoe to Kou, with another stroke he passed to Waianae, and then began to fish from the shore far out to the sea, using a round, deep net. This method of fishing continues to the present day. A fish is caught and a weight tied to it so that it must swim slowly. Other fish come to see the stranger, and the net is drawn around them. Many good fish were caught, but the great fish did not come. Again Kawelo came to hunt this Uhumakaikai, but the Uhu sent fierce storm-waves against the canoe to drive it to land. Kawelo held the boat strongly with his paddle. Soon the Uhu appeared, trying to strike the boat and upset it. Kawelo and his fisherman carefully watched every move and balanced the boat as needed. Kawelo's net was in the water, its mouth open, and its full length dragging far behind the boat. The Uhu was swimming around the net as if despising its every motion, but Kawelo swept the net sideways and the fish found himself swimming into the net. Kawelo swiftly rushed the net forward until the Uhu was fully enclosed. Then came a marvellous fish-battle. The waves swept high around the boat. Kawelo and the fisherman covered it so that the water poured off rather than into it. Then the Uhu swam swiftly out into the blue waters. The fisherman begged Kawelo to cut the cord which held the net. Far out they went—out to the most distant island, Niihau. Kawelo saw a great battle in the net which held the Uhu. There were many fish inside attacking the Uhu. They were a kind of whiskered fish, biting like rats, digging their teeth into the flesh of the great fish. Kawelo uttered incantations, and the fish became weaker and weaker until it ceased to struggle. Kawelo paddled with strong strokes back to Oahu.

Meanwhile the brothers and parents, who had gone to Kauai, were in great trouble under the persecutions of Aikanaka and his strong man Kauahoa. At last the mother sent the brothers to Oahu after Kawelo. They came to Waikiki while Kawelo was away trying to kill the Uhu. The youngest brother, Kamalama, received them and sent two messengers to find Kawelo. He recited a family chant, in which the names of the visiting brothers as well as the name of Kawelo's gods were honored. He charged them to remember the brothers' names or they would have trou-

ble. They paddled out on the ocean calling for
Kawelo and repeating the names from time to
time. Suddenly a high surf wave caught their
canoe and overturned it, leaving them to struggle in the fierce waters. Soon they saw Kawelo
coming with his great fish near his canoe. "O
Kawelo!" they cried. "We had the names of your
friends from Kauai—but our trouble in the
water made us forget." Then Kawelo recited his
chant, giving his brothers' names and also those
of the tabu gods. Only the chiefs to whom the
gods belonged could speak their names. When
Kawelo uttered their names, the two men cried
out, "Those are the men, and Kuka-lani-ehu is
their god." Kawelo was very angry at the dese-
cration of the name of his family god in the
mouths of the common men. He stuck his paddle deep into the sea, tearing the coral reef to
pieces, but the great fish caught on the coral and
Kawelo could not row to the men. They rushed
their boat to the beach and escaped. Kawelo
then took a part of the captured fish and offered
it for sacrifice in the temple at Waianae. The rest
he brought to his people at Waikiki.

As he came near the shore he called for his
spear-throwers to meet him on the beach. Seven
skilled men stood before him as he landed. They
hurled their spears at one time straight at him,
but he moved himself skilfully from side to side

and threw the ends of his malo (loincloth) around them and caught them all together. Then he called his two adopted boys to throw. This they did with great skill, but he caught both spears in one hand. Kamalama took two spears, and Kawelo's wife stood on one side with a fishhook and line in her hand. As the spears flew by her she threw out the hook and caught each one.

The story of the Kauai trouble was soon told. The king of Oahu furnished a large double canoe. From his father-in-law Kawelo secured the historic battle-weapons—war-club and spear —with which he had learned to fight. Food in abundance was placed on the boats, and the household went back to Kauai to wage war with Aikanaka and Kauahoa, stopping at the heiau Kamaile—afterward called Ka-ne i ka pua lena (Ka-ne of the yellow flower)—to offer sacrifices. Some legends say this temple was at Makaha, and that Kane-aki was the name. This Ka-ne was one of the gods of Kawelo. Kawelo, according to one legend, had his people tie him in a mat as if dead as they approached Wailua, the home of Aikanaka. The beach was covered with people—the warriors of Aikanaka. As the double canoe came to the beach, the people made ready to attack. They waited, however, for the newcomers to land and prepare for fight. This was a formal courtesy always demanded by the ethics of olden times. When all was ready, Kamalama stood by the apparently dead body of Kawelo, and pulled a cord which unloosed the mats. Kawelo rose up with his war-club and spear in hand and rushed upon the multitude. He struck from side to side, and the people fell like the leaves of trees in a whirlwind.

Again new bodies of warriors hastened from Aikanaka. Kamalama, the seven spearmen and the two adopted boys fought this army and drove it back under a cliff where Aikanaka had his headquarters. The seven spearmen, known in the legends as Naulu (the-seven-bread-fruit-trees), were afraid and retreated to the boat.

Two noble chiefs asked Aikanaka for two large bodies of men (two four-hundreds), but Kawelo and his handful of helpers defeated them with great slaughter. Thus several larger bodies of soldiers were destroyed, and Aikanaka became cold and afraid in his heart.

Then Kahakaloa, the best skilled in the use of war-clubs in all the islands, rose up and went down with the two hundred warriors to fight with Kawelo and his family. The father-in-law of Kawelo knew this chief well and thought that by him Kawelo might be killed if he went to Kauai, but Kawelo had learned strokes of the club not understood on Kauai. Soon all the warriors were slain, and Kahakaloa stood alone against Kawelo. As they faced each other Kahakaloa swiftly struck Kawelo, but Kawelo while falling gave his club an upward stroke, breaking his enemy's arm. In the next struggle Kawelo's swift upward stroke killed his foe.

Then Kauahoa, the strongest, tallest and most skilful man of Kauai, arose and went down to meet Kawelo. Kauahoa took a magic koa-tree, root, stem and branches, for his club with which to fight Kawelo. His heart was full of anger as he remembered the troubles between Kawelo and himself in their boyhood. As he passed the multitude of his dead people he became beside himself with rage and rushed upon Kawelo. Kawelo stationed his wife on one side with her powerful fishhooks and lines to catch the branches of the mighty tree and hold them fast. Some of the legends say that she was very skilful in the use of the ikoi. This was a straight, somewhat heavy, stick with a strong cord fastened around the middle. It was said that she was to throw this stick over the branches, whirling and twisting the cord around them, greatly entangling them, so that she could pull the tree to one side. Kawelo ordered his warriors to watch the spots of sunlight sifting through the branches. As the tree was hurled down upon them they must leap into the open places and seize the branches, holding on as best they could. When the giant struck down with his strange war-club, Kawelo's friends followed his directions, while he leaped swiftly to one side and ran around back of Kauahoa while he was bending over trying to free his tree from its troubles. Kawelo struck down with awful force, his war-club cutting Kauahoa in pieces, which fell by the side of the koa-tree.

Somewhere in the battles waged by Kawelo along the coasts of Kauai he was fighting with his giant enemy and struck his spear against the mountain ridge at Anahola, piercing it through and through, leaving a great hole through which the sky is always to be seen.

Aikanaka fled to the region near Hanapepe, where he dwelt in poverty. Kawelo divided the districts of Kauai among his warriors. Kaeleha received the district in which Aikanaka was sheltered. Soon this adopted son of Kawelo met the daughter of Aikanaka and married her. After a while he wanted Aikanaka to again rule the island. He proposed rebellion and told Aikanaka that they could destroy Kawelo because he had never learned the art of fighting with stones. He only understood the use of the war-club and spear. They ordered the women and children to gather great piles of stones to hurl against Kawelo.

When Kawelo heard about this insurrection, he was very angry. He seized his war-club,

Kuikaa, and hastened to Hanapepe. As he came near he saw that the people had barricaded his way with canoes, and that back of these canoes were many large piles of stones in the care of warriors. He raised his war-club and leaped toward his enemies. A sling-stone reached him. Then the stones came like heavy rain. He dodged, but there were so many that when he avoided one he would be struck by others. He was bruised and wounded and stunned until he sank to the ground unconscious under the fierce shower.

The people rejoiced, and, to make death sure, threw off the stones and beat the body with clubs until it was cold and they could detect no sign of breathing.

Aikanaka had built a new unu, or heiau, at Mauilli, in the district of Koloa, but no man had been offered as a sacrifice upon its altars. He thought he would take Kawelo as the first human sacrifice. The people carried the body of Kawelo to the pa, or outside enclosure, of the temple, but it was dark when they arrived, and they laid the body down, covering it with banana leaves, saying they would come the next morning and place the body on the altar, where it should lie until decomposition had taken place.

Two watchmen had been appointed, one of whom was a near relative to Kawelo. He soon

discovered that Kawelo was not dead. He told
Kawelo about the plan to place him on the altar
in the morning. He covered Kawelo again, placing his war-club by his side. In the morning the
chiefs and people came to the heiau with
Aikanaka and Kaeleha. When all were gathered
together the watchman whispered to Kawelo.
The leaves were thrown off, and Kawelo
attacked the multitude and destroyed all who
had rebelled against him.

Some of the legends say that Aikanaka had
placed Kawelo on the sacrificial platform and in
the morning had begun to offer the prayer consecrating the dead body to the gods, when
Kawelo struck him dead before his own altar.

When this rebellion had been overcome,
Kawelo gave a large district with good lands to
the watchman who had befriended him. He
retained his younger brother Kamalama in the
district of Hanamaulu and committed their
parents to his care.

Kawelo, as was his right, ruled over all the
island, passing from place to place, establishing
peace and prosperity. He made his home at
Hana, planting and fishing for himself, not bur-
dening chiefs or people, but beloved by all.
Thus he gained the honored name Kawelo-lei-
makua (Kawelo, garland-of-his-parents).

Chapter 23

"CHIEF MAN-EATER"

"Chief Man-eater," the cannibal, lived in the Hawaiian Islands. He was also one of the inhabitants of mistland. Legends gathered around him like clouds. Facts also stood out like tall trees through the clouds. He was a real cannibal, of whom the Hawaiians are not proud.

The Hawaiians have frequently been called cannibals. Secretaries of the Missionary Board under which the first missionaries came to Hawaii, and papers of the denomination supporting that mission, have uttered the untruth, "The cannibals of the Sandwich Islands would erewhile cook and carve a merchant or marine and discourse on the deliciousness of cold missionary." It was a very forcible background against which to paint moral improvement, but it was not accurate. The Hawaiians claim that they never practised cannibalism. If anything like a feast of human flesh was partaken of, it was only in exceedingly rare and obscure cases.

And of these only "Chief Man-eater" is accepted as a historical fact. Legends that possibly have had a hint of cannibalism are very few.

It is recorded that after certain fierce battles of the long ago, as a method of showing indignity to dead chiefs, their bodies were baked and thrown into the sea.

It is barely possible that the baking was followed by cannibalism, but there is nothing in the record beyond the suggestion.

The daring act of "heart-eating" is mentioned in Hawaiian annals. This came during or after a battle, when two warriors had been engaged in a hand-to-hand struggle. The victor, whose strength was almost gone, would sometimes tear out the heart of the dying opponent and eat it on the spot. It was believed that the strength and courage of the dead entered immediately into the living.

That the Hawaiian chiefs and priests set small value upon life is well attested by the large number of human sacrifices required for almost all civil and religious ceremonies. For instance, when the famous war-god Kaili was taken to a temple dedicated to it by Kamehameha, eleven human victims were placed at once upon the altar before it. When a chief desired a new canoe a man was usually slain at the foot of the tree from which the canoe was to be made. Another was slain when the canoe was complete, and others might be sacrificed at different stages of the work. When a chief's house was to be erected, sometimes a victim was sacrificed and buried at each corner, and when the house was completed another slaughter occurred. When an idol was to be made, substantially the same sacrifices accompanied the ceremony of choosing the tree and carving the image. At certain times the priests of all the temples demanded human victims, and regularly appointed officers, or man-catchers, were appointed to provide for the sacrifice. Not even their own relatives were spared in the search. Women were almost always exempt from this horrible termination of life. When a battle had been fought, many captives were sacrificed by both victor and vanquished.

Infanticide was freely practised up to the time of the advent of the missionaries. Even for old people there was often but little love, and the aged and the infirm were left to care for themselves, or placed on the beach for the outstretched hands of the incoming tide.

A native historian says: "The ancient restrictions of chiefs and priests were like the poisoned tooth of a reptile. If the shadow of a common man fell on a chief, it was death. If he put on any part of the garments of a chief, it was death. If he went into the chief's yard or upon the chief's house, it was death. If he stood when the king's bathing water or his garments were carried along, or in the king's presence, it was death. If he stood at the mention of the king's name in song, it was death. There were many other offences of the people which were made capital by the chiefs. The king and the priests were much alike. The priesthood was oppressive to the people. Human victims were required on many occasions. If tabus were violated it meant death. It was death to be found in a canoe on a tabu or sacred day. If a woman ate pork, coconuts, bananas, or certain kind of fish or lobster, it was death."

This much, and more, of human cruelty is acknowledged concerning the savage life of ancient Hawaii. Nevertheless, from the beginning of the earliest acquaintance of white people with the Hawaiian not an instance or hint of cannibalism has been known.

The idea of eating human flesh was thoroughly repugnant. Alexander, in his brief history of the Hawaiian people, says, "Cannibalism was regarded with horror and detestation." Isaac Davis, one of the first white men to make his home in the islands, declared that the Hawaiians had never been cannibals since the islands were inhabited.

To the Hawaiian, "Chief Man-eater" was the unique and horrid embodiment of an insane appetite. He was the "Fe-fi-fo-fum" giant of the Hawaiian nursery. The very thought of his worse than brutal feast made the Hawaiian blood run cold.

One of the legends of Ke-alii-ai Kanaka (The-chief-who-eats-men) tells of the sudden appearance on the island of Kauai, in the indefinite past, of a stranger chief from a foreign land, with a small band of followers. The king of Kauai made them welcome. Feasts and games were enjoyed, then came the discovery that secret feasts of a horrible nature were eaten by the strangers. They were driven from the island. They crossed the channel to Oahu. They knew their reputation would soon follow them, so they went inland to the lofty range of the Waianae Mountains. Here they established their home, cultivated food and captured human victims, until finally driven out. Then they launched their boats and sailed away toward Kahiki, a foreign land.

Ai-Kanaka (Man-eater) was the name given to a bay on the island of Molokai, now known as the leper island. Here dwelt the priest Kawelo, who, by the aid of the great shark-god Kauhuhu, brought upon his enemies a storm which swept them into the sea, where they were eaten by the subjects and companions of the shark-god.

A legend, or, rather, a genealogy, placed a "Chief Man-eater" on the island of Hawaii, but no hints are given of man-eating feasts, or of journeys to other islands, and the name may simply refer to a fierce disposition. The Oahu chief, Ke-alii-ai Kanaka, lived some time about the middle of the eighteenth century, as nearly as can be estimated. Up to the middle of the nineteenth century the accounts of Chief Man-eater's deeds and the accurate knowledge of his place of residence were quite fresh in the minds of old Hawaiians.

It is still a problem to be decided whether Chief Man-eater was a foreigner or a Hawaiian. The difficulty that makes his foreign birth a problem is the accepted date of the close of all intercourse with far-away island groups, such as Samoa and Fiji—at least three hundred years earlier than the century assigned to Ke-alii-ai Kanaka.

It would seem best to accept the legend that the degenerate chief was a desperado and an outcast from the high chief family of Waialua, on the northwest coast of Oahu.

Ke-alii-ai Kanaka was a powerful man. He is described as a champion boxer and wrestler. In some way he learned to love the taste of human flesh. When his awful appetite became known he was driven from his home. As he passed through the village the women who had been his playmates and companions fled from him. His former friends, the young warriors, called out "Man-eater! Man-eater!" and openly despised him. In bitter anger he called the few servants who would follow him, and fled to the royal Waianae Mountains. Driven from his kindred and friends, he buried himself and his brutal appetite in the mountain forests.

It is possible that soon after this he visited the island Kauai, and there passed himself off as a chief from a foreign land. But "his hand was against every man" and therefore "every man's hand was against him." Finally he made his permanent home among the Waianae Mountains, in the range that borders Waialua.

His followers numbered only a handful, for a single canoe brought them away from Kauai—if his was indeed the band driven from the hospitable shores of that fertile island.

Kokoa and Kalo were the names by which he was known in his nobler young manhood, and Kokoa was his name to his followers, but he was ever after Chief Man-eater to the Hawaiian world.

It was a wild and wonderfully beautiful spot that Kokoa chose for his final home. It was a small plateau, or mesa, of from two to three hundred acres on the top of a small mountain surrounded by other higher and more precipitous cliffs. It was luxuriantly covered with tropical growth and blessed with abundant rains. The Hawaiians have given the name Halemanu (house-of-the-hand) to this plateau. Its sides, sloping down into the valleys, were so precipitous as to be absolutely inaccessible. It could be entered only along a narrow ridge. The pandanus drooped its long leaves and aërial rootlets along the edges. The uluhe,* or tangle-fern, massed and matted itself into a thick disguise for the cannibals' secret paths through the valleys below. Native flowers bordered the paths and crowned the plateau, as if man's worst nature could never wither the appeal of things beautiful. A magnificent koa, or native mahogany, tree spread its protecting branches by the spot chosen by Kokoa for his grass house. Kukui-trees furnished their oily nuts for his torches. The ohia, or native apple, and the bread-fruit and wild sugar-cane gave generously of their wealth to the support of the cannibal band. They easily cultivated taro, the universal native food, and captured birds and sometimes unwary hunters who penetrated the forest recesses in search of the birds with rare yellow feathers. It was a beautiful den into which, spider-like, he dragged his victims.

Kokoa led his followers into the mountains

* Gleichenia longissima.

through winding valleys and thick forests and sometimes in the very beds of the Waianae brooks to this secluded retreat lying within the walls of one of the enormous extinct craters of the volcanic mountains. As they entered the valley below the plateau, one of his followers said to another: "Our chief has found a true hiding-place for us. Let us hope that it may not prove a trap. If our presence here should be known to the people of Waialua, they could easily close the entrance to this valley with a strong guard and drive us against the steep walls up which we cannot climb." Kokoa only called out, "Wait, I will protect you," then led them to the plateau he had selected.

The ascent to the summit was along a knife-blade ridge flanked by picturesque sides. For a long distance there was only room for one man to walk. One of the men carelessly hastened across this causeway, bearing a heavy burden of goods and weapons. His foot slipped. His burden overbalanced him. The sloping side of the ridge was covered with grass, which afforded no foothold. In a moment the fallen man and his burden were hurled down the slope. The terrified friends watched the flying body in its rapid descent, and saw it shoot out in space over the edge of a lava cliff, and heard it strike the broken debris at the foot.

Two of the men were at once sent back to skirt the cliff and secure the remains of their companion. The others followed Kokoa with more careful steps.

This hill, crowned by table-land, which was to be their home, was apparently the very centre of volcanic activity in former days. It had been the deposit of the last traces of the crater. Lava and ashes had been piled up, and then when the fires died away had been coated with the island plant life. Here they found a fortress that could not be assailed or approached except by one man at a time. From this place raids could be easily made upon the surrounding country. Here they brought their captives for their inhuman feasts.

After the grass houses were built for permanent shelter, Kokoa (Ke-alii-ai Kanaka) caused a great hole to be made. This was the imu, or oven, in which the bodies of animals and men were to be baked. A fire was built in the bottom of the hole. Stones were placed upon the burning wood. When these stones were thoroughly heated and the fire had died away, the bodies were wrapped in fragrant and spicy leaves, laid upon the stones, and covered so that the heat might not escape. Then water was carefully poured down so that clouds of steam might make tender the flesh roasting over the heated stones. This was the ordinary Hawaiian method of preparing fish or chickens or animals for their numerous feasts.* It was the regular festival preparation required by the cannibals.

After a time Kokoa and his companions took a huge outcropping block of lava and smoothed away the top, making a hollow ipukai, or table dish, or, more literally, a gravy dish, upon which their ghastly repasts were served. This stone table was finally rounded and its sides ornamented by rudely carved figures. The stone was five or six feet in circumference. Not far from it the chief's grass house was built and the ground prepared for the taro which should be their daily food.

Sometimes members of the little band carried birds which had been cunningly snared, and exchanged them for fish and chickens with families living on the seashore. Frequently the entire band would make an attack upon a lonely household and carry every member of it to the mountain lair, that day after day they might be provided with such food as would satisfy the shameless craving of their gross appetites.

The cannibal band often met strong resistance, and with their captives carried back the dead bodies of their friends. Sickness and death occasionally crossed the narrow ridge and

* Luau.

199

struck down some of Chief Man-eater's follow-ers, until at last Ke-alii-ai Kanaka stood alone by the ipukai.

Alone he watched for hunters and for those who came searching for rare plants or woods or birds. He guarded well his solitary retreat on the tableland. He did many daring deeds and terrified the people by his fabulous strength and courage.

One day he captured and killed a victim whom he carried through the forest to Halemanu.

A brother of this victim discovered and fol-lowed him to the path along the ridge. He rec-ognized the chief who had been driven long before from Waialua. He knew the reputation for boxing and wrestling which belonged to his former leader. He went back to his village. For a year Hoahanau gave himself up to athletic training. He sought the strong men—the boxers and wrestlers of Waialua. He visited other parts of the island until he found no one who could stand before him. Then alone he sought the hid-ing-place of Chief Man-eater. He covered his lithe and sinewy body with oil, that his enemy might not easily grasp an arm or limb. He reached the narrow pass leading to Halemanu.

His challenge rang out, and Chief Man-eater came forth to meet him. The chief started along the narrow path swinging a heavy war club and flourishing a long spear.

Hoahanau made himself known and was recognized by the chief. Then Hoahanau made known the terms upon which he wished to wrestle with the chief.

"Take back your club and spear, and stand unarmed beside your ipukai, and I will also stand unarmed by your imu. No weapon shall be near our hands. Then will we wrestle for the mastery."

Aikanaka despised Hoahanau, whose strength he had well known in the past. He believed that he could easily overcome the daring man who stood naked before him; therefore, boastfully taunting Hoahanau and threatening to eat his body upon that very ipukai, he threw away his weapons and waited the onset.

As the combatants threw themselves against each other, Aikanaka was surprised to find his antagonist ready for every cunning feint and well-timed blow. It was a long and fearful struggle. The chief had been once thrown to the ground, but had twisted aside and regained his feet before Hoahanau could take advantage of the fall.

Foaming at the mouth and roaring and screaming like an enraged animal, Aikanaka turned for a second toward his house, with the thought of rushing to secure a weapon. Then Hoahanau leaped upon him, caught him, and whirled him over the edge of the plateau. Down the chief swept, broken and mangled by the rough, sharp spurs of lava rock, until the lifeless body lodged in the branches of a tall ohia-tree far below.

Note: This was the beginning and ending of cannibalism in the Hawaiian Islands so far as history and definite legend are concerned. Hale-manu was visited by Mathison, and a description of the carved stone table published in 1825.

In 1848, a little party of white men were guided to the crater by an old Hawaiian, who repeated to them the story of "Chief Man-eater" substantially as it is given in this record. They found Halemanu. The foundations of the house, or at least of a wall around it, were easily traced. The ipukai and the imu were both there. The party did not notice any carved images on the side of the stone table. Indeed, the stone had been so covered by decaying debris that it scarcely extended a foot above the soil.

In 1879 and in 1890, Mr. D. D. Baldwin, a member of the party visiting Halemanu in 1848, again sought the ipukai without a guide, but the luxuriant growth of tangle-fern and grass made exploration difficult, and the carved stone table was not found. Somewhere under the debris of Halemanu it may wait the patient search of a Hawaiian archaeologist.

Mr. Joseph Emerson, who has had charge of governmental surveys of a large part of the islands and also is a prominent authority on Hawaiian matters, says that the sacrificial stone can still be found, and was seen by his brother within the past few years. He differs from the other writers in the name given to the place and also in regard to the locality. The right name should be "Helemano," carrying the idea of a train of followers of some high chief. The locality is some miles northwest of the Waianae Range in one of the valleys of the Koolau Mountains. To this place the chiefesses of highest blood were wont to come for the birth of their expected children. The valley was "tabu" or "sacred." Near this sacred birthplace of chiefs was the home for a time of the noted man-eating chief.

Chapter 24

LEPE-A-MOA

THE CHICKEN-GIRL OF PALAMA

Strange things are sometimes imagined in the Hawaiian legends of ancient time. The story of Lepe-a-moa is an illustration of the blending of the Hawaiian idea of supernatural things with the deeds of every-day life. It is one of those old legends handed down by native bards through generations, whose first scenes lie on the island of Kauai, but change to Oahu.

Keahua was one of the royal chiefs of Kauai. Apparently he was the highest chief on the island, but it was in the days when men were few and high chiefs and gods were many. He had spent his boyhood on the rich lands of Wailua, Kauai, and from there had crossed the deep channel to Oahu and had come to the home of the chiefess Kapa-lama after her beautiful daughter Kauhao, to take her to Kauai as his wife. But soon after his return one of the kupua gods became angry with him. A kupua was a god having a double body, sometimes appearing as a man and sometimes as an animal. The animal body always possessed supernatural powers.

This kupua was called Akua-pehu-ale (god-of-the-swollen-billows). He devoured his enemies, and was greatly feared and hated even by his own tribe. He attacked Keahua, destroyed his people and drove him into the forests far up the mountain-sides, where, at a place called Kawai-kini (The-many-waters), where fresh spring water abounded, the chief gathered his followers together and built a new home.

One day Kapalama, who was living in her group of houses in the part of Honolulu which now bears her name, said to her husband: "O Honouliuli, our daughter on Kauai will have a child of magic power and of kupua character. Perhaps we should go thither, adopt it, and bring it up; there is life in the bones."

They crossed the channel, carrying offerings with them to their gods. Concealing their canoes, they went up into the forest. Their daughter's child was already born, and behold, it was only an egg! The chief had given an order to carry, it out into the deep sea and throw it away as an offering to the sea-monsters; but the mother and her soothsayers thought it should be kept and brought to life.

Kapalama, coming at this time, took the egg, wrapped it carefully in soft kapas, bade farewell to her daughter, and returned to Oahu. Here she had her husband build a fine thatched house of the best grass he could gather. The kapas put inside for beds and clothing were perfumed by fragrant ginger flowers, hala blossoms, and the delicate bloom of the niu (coconut) while festoons of the sweet-scented maile graced its walls. For a long time that egg lay wrapped in its coverings of soft kapas.

One day Kapalama told her husband to prepare an imu (oven) for their grandchild. He gathered stones, dug a hole, and took his fire-sticks and rubbed until fire came; then he built a fire in the hole and placed the wood and put on the stones, heating them until they were very hot. Taking some fine sweet-potatoes, he wrapped them in leaves and laid the bundles on the stones, covered all with mats, and poured on sufficient water to make steam in which to cook the potatoes.

When all was fully cooked, Kapalama went to the house of the egg and looked in. There she saw a wonderfully beautiful chicken born from that egg. The feathers were of all the colors of all kinds of birds. They named the bird-child Lepe-a-moa. They fed it fragments of the cooked sweet-potato, and it went to sleep, putting its head under its wing.

This bird-child had an ancestress who was a bird-woman and who lived up in the air in the

highest clouds. Her name was Ke-ao-lewa (The-
moving-cloud). She was a sorceress of the sky,
but sometimes came to earth in the form of a
great bird, or of a woman, to aid her relatives in
various ways. When the egg was brought from
Kauai, Ke-ao-lewa told her servants to prepare a
swimming-pool for the use of the child. After
this bird-child had come into her new life and
eaten and rested, she went to the edge of the
pool, ruffled and picked her feathers and drank
of sweet water, then leaped in, swimming and
diving and splashing all around the pool. When
tired of this play, she got out and flew up in the
branches of a tree, shaking off the water and
drying herself. After a little while she flew down
to her sleeping-house, wrapped herself in some
fine, soft kapas, and went to sleep.

Thus day by day she ate and bathed, and,
when by herself she changed her bird form into
that of a very beautiful girl, her body shone with
beauty like the red path of the sunlight on the
sea, or the rainbow bending in the sky.

One day after she had made this change she
stretched herself out with her face downward
and called to her grandparents: "Oh, where are
you two? Perhaps you will come inside."

They heard a weak, muffled voice, and one
said: "Where is that voice calling us two? This
is a strange thing. As a tabu place, no one has

been allowed to come here; it is for us and our children alone." The woman said, "We will listen again; perhaps we can understand this voice." Soon they heard the child call as before. Kapalama said: "That is a voice from the house of our child. We must go there."

She ran to the house, lifted the mat door, and looked in. When she saw a beautiful and strong girl lying on the floor she was overcome with surprise, and staggered back and fell to the ground as if dead. Honouliuli ran to her, rubbed her body, poured water on her head and brought her back to life. Then she said: "When I looked in, I saw our grandchild in a beautiful human body wearing a green and yellow feather lei. It was her voice calling us."

Thus Lepe-a-moa came into her two bodies and received her gift of magic powers. She was exceedingly beautiful as a gift, so beautiful that her glory shone out from her body like radiating fire, filling the house and passing through into the mist around, shining in that mist in resplendent rainbow colors. The radiance was around her wherever she went.

One day she said to her grandparents, "I want another kind of food, and am going down to the sea for fish and moss." In her chicken body she ate the potato food provided, but she desired the food of her friends when in her human form. Joyously she went down to the shore and saw the surf waves of Palama roiling in. She chanted as she saw this white surf: "My love, the first surf. I ride on these white waves."

As she rested on the crest of a great comber sweeping toward the beach she saw a squid rising up and tossing out its long arms to catch her. She laughed and caught it in her hand, saying, "One squid, the first, for the gods." This she took to the beach and put in a fish-basket she had left on the sand with her skirt and lei. Again she went out, and saw two squid rising to meet her. This time she sang, "Here are two squid for the grandparents." Then she saw and caught another floating on the wave with her. This she took, exclaiming, "For me; this squid is mine."

The grandparents rejoiced when they saw the excellent food provided them. Again and again she went to the sea, catching fish and gathering sweet moss from the reef. Thus the days of her childhood passed. Her grandfather gave his name, Honouliuli, to a land district west of Honolulu, while Kapalama gave hers to the place where they lived. The bird-child's parents still dwelt in their forest home on Kauai, hidden from their enemy Akua-pehu-ale.

Note: In Hawaiian legends and even in history, down to the last ruler of the islands, a divinely given rainbow was supposed to be arched from time to time over those of high-chief birth. A child of divine and human or miraculous power in the family of a high chief would almost invariably have its birth attended by thunder, lightning, storm, and brilliant rainbows. These rainbows would usually follow the child wherever it went, resting over any place where it stopped. Sometimes the glory of the royal blood in a child would be so great that it would shine through the thatch of a house like a blazing fire, flashing out in the darkness like devouring flames, or, if the child was in the sea, the glory shone into the spray like rainbows.

Some legends state that the sorcerers could tell the difference between the colors radiating from members of different royal families. If a kahuna saw a canoe far away with a mass of color above it, he could give the name of the person in it and his lineage. It is even stated that it was possible to discern these rainbows of royalty from island to island and know where the person was at that time staying. Lono-o-pua-kau was the god who had charge of these signs of a chief's presence.

Kauilani and Akua-pehu-ale

After a time Lepe-a-moa's mother gave birth to a fine boy, who was named Kauilani. He was born in the forest by the water-springs Kawaikini. On the day of his birth a great storm swept over the land. Rain fell in torrents and swept in red streams down the valleys, thunder rolled, lightning flashed, earthquakes shook the land, and rainbows arched his birthplace. This time, since a boy was born, he belonged to the family of the father. His grandparents were Lau-ka-ie-ie and Kani-a-ula.

They took the child and bathed him in a wonderful fountain called Wai-ui (Water-of-strength), which had the power of conferring rapid growth, great strength, and remarkable beauty upon those who bathed therein. The child was taken frequently to this fountain, so that he grew rapidly and was soon a man with only the years of a boy. The two old people were kupuas having very great powers. They could appear as human beings or could assume wind bodies and fly like the wind from place to place. They could not give the boy a double body, but they could give him supernatural powers with his name Kauilani (The-divine-athlete). They bound around him their marvellous malo (loin cloth) called Paihiku.

211

When Keahua, the father, saw the boy, he said: "How is it that you have grown so fast and become a man so soon? Life is with you. Perhaps now you can help me. A quarrelsome friend sought war with me a long time ago and came near killing me; that is why we dwell in this mountain forest beyond his reach. Maybe you and my servants can destroy this enemy," telling him also the character and dwelling-place of Akua-pehu-ale.

Kauilani said to his father, "If you adopt my plan, perhaps we may kill this Akua-pehu-ale." The father agreed and asked what steps should be taken. He was then told to send his servants up into the mountain to cut down ahakea*-trees and shape them into planks, then carry some of the sticks to the foot of the precipice near their home, and set them in the ground and to take the others to the sea and there set them up like stakes close together.

That night was made very dark by the sorcery of the young chief. All the people slept soundly. At midnight Kauilani went out into the darkness and called thus to his gods:

"O mountain! O sea! O South! O North! O all ye gods! Come to our aid! Inland at the foot of the pali is the ahakea; by the sea stands the ahakea, there by the beach of Hina. Multiply

* Bobea Elatior also Hookeri.

212

them with the wauke at the foot of the pail of Halelea and by the shore of Wailua. Bananas are ready for us this night. The bread-fruit and the sugar-cane are ours, O ye gods!"

Repeating this incantation, he went into his house and slept. In the morning the high chief, Keahua, went out and looked, and behold! the sticks planted below the precipice had taken root and sent out branches and intertwined until it spread an almost impenetrable thicket. There were also many groups of wauke-trees which had sprung up in the night. He called his wife, saying, "While we slept, this wonderful thing has transpired."

Kauilani came out and asked his father to call all the people and have them go out and cut the bark from the wauke-trees, beat it into kapa, and spread it out to dry. This was quickly done, and two large houses also built and finished the same day. A tabu of silence was claimed for the night while he again petitioned the gods.

Soon deep darkness rested on the land, and all the people fell asleep, for they were very tired. Kauilani only remained awake at his incantations, listening to the rapid work of the gods in cutting trees, carving images, and filling the houses with them.

Awaking the next day, the chief and his people went to the houses and saw they were filled to overflowing with images, and covering the platforms and fences around the houses.

Kauilani said to his father, "Let the men go up to a high hill inland and burn the dry wood and brush to attract the attention of your enemy while we prepare our battle."

Akua-pehu-ale was sporting in the sea when he saw the smoke rising from the hills and mingling with the clouds. He said: "That is something different from a cloud, and must be smoke from a fire made by some man. What man has escaped my eyes? I will go and see, and when I find him he shall be food for me." Then he came to the beach, and his magic body flew to the lands below Kawaikini.

All the people had been concealed by Kanilani, who alone remained to face the sea-monster. He stood in the doorway of one of the two large houses, with an image on each side, for which he had made eyes looking like those of a man.

The god came up, and, fixing his eyes on the young chief, said: "Why are you hiding here? You have escaped in the past, but now you shall become my food." He opened his mouth wide, one jaw rising up like a precipice, the other resting on the ground, his double-pointed tongue playing swiftly and leaping to swallow the chief and the images by his side.

Kauilani said sternly, "Return to your place to-day, and you shall see my steps toward your place to-morrow for battle."

The god hesitated, and then said: "Sweet is the fatness of this place. Your bones are soft, your skin is shining. The glory of your body this day shall cease."

The chief, without making any motion, replied: "Wait a little; perhaps this means work for us two. This is my place. If I strike you, you may be my food, and the pieces of your body and your lands and property may fall to me like raindrops. It may be best that you should die, for you are very old, your eyelids hang down, and your skin is dry like that of an unihipili god [a god of skin and bones]. But I am young. This is not the day for our fight. To-morrow we can have our contest. Return to your sea beach; to-morrow I will go down."

The god thought a moment, and, knowing that the word of a chief was pledged for a battle, decided that he would return to a better place for a victory, so turned and went back to the shore.

The young chief at once called his father and the people, and said: "To-morrow I am going down to fight with our enemy. Perhaps he will kill me; if so, glorious will be my death for you; but I would ask you to command the people to eat until satisfied, lest they be exhausted in the battle to-morrow; then let them sleep."

He laid out his plan of battle and defence. His mother and the grandparents who had cared for him, with a number of the people, were to fight protected by the growth of trees at the foot of the pali, and were to turn the god and his people toward the houses filled with the wooden gods made by the aumakuas (the ghost-gods).

While all slept, Kauilani went out into the darkness and prayed to the thousands of the multitude of gods to work and establish his power from dawn until night.

In the morning he girded around him his malo of magic power and made ready to go down. His father came to him with a polished spear, its end shaped to a sharp point, and set it up between them, saying: "This spear is an ancestor of yours. It has miraculous power and can tell you what to do. Its name is Koa-wi Koa-wa. It now belongs to you to care for you and fight for you." The young chief gratefully took the spear and then said to his father: "Your part is to be watchman in the battle to-day. If the smoke of the conflict rises to the sky and then sweeps seaward and at last comes before you, you may know that I am dead; but if the smoke rises to the foot of the precipice and passes along to the great houses, you may know that the enemy is slain."

Then Kauilani took his spear and went down to the open field near the shore, talking all the way to it and to the gods. When he came to the seashore, he saw the god rising up like a mighty dragon, roaring and making a noise like reverberating thunder. As he rushed upon the chief, there was the sound as of great surf-waves beating on the beach. The sand and soil of the battlefield was tossed up in great clouds. The god fought in his animal body, which was that of a great, swollen sea-monster.

Kauilani whirled his sharp-edged spear with swift bird's-wing movement, chanting meanwhile: "O Koa-wi Koa-wa, strike! Strike for the lives of us two! Strike!" The power of his magic girdle strengthened his arms, and the spear was ready to act in harmony with every thought of its chief. It struck the open mouth of that god, and turned it toward the precipice and thick trees. Backward it was forced by the swift strokes of the spear. When a rush was made, the chief leaped toward the pali, and thus the god was driven and lured away from his familiar surroundings. He became tangled in the thickets, and was harassed by the attacks of Kauilani's friends.

At last his face was turned toward the houses filled with gods. The power which all the ghost gods had placed in the images of wood was now descending upon Akua-pehu-ale, and he began to grow weak rapidly. He felt the loss of strength, and turned to make a desperate rush upon the young chief.

Kauilani struck him a heavy blow, and the spear leaped again and again upon him, till he rolled into a mountain stream at a place called Kapaa, out of which he crawled almost drowned. Then he was driven along even to the image houses, where a fierce battle took place, in which the wooden images took part, many of them being torn to pieces by the teeth of Akua-pehu-ale.

Some legends say that Kanilani's ancestress, Ke-ao-lewa, who had watched over his sister, the bird-child, Lepe-a-moa, had come from her home in the clouds to aid in the defeat of Akua-pehu-ale.

All forces uniting drove their enemy into a great, mysterious cloud of mana, or miraculous power, and he fell dead under a final blow of the cutting spear Koa-wi Koa-wa. Then Kanilani and his warriors rolled the dead body into one of the large houses. There he offered a chant of worship and of sacrifice, consecrating it as an offering to all the gods who had aided him in his battle.

When this ceremony was over he set fire to the houses and burned the body of Akua-pehu-ale and all the wooden images which remained after the conflict, the smoke of which rose up and swept along the foot of the precipice.

The father saw this, and told his people that the young chief had killed their enemy, so with great rejoicing they prepared a feast for the victorious chief and his helpers.

Kanilani went with his parents and grandparents down to the shore and took possession of all that part of the island around Wailua, comprising large fish-ponds, and taro and sweet-potato lands, held by the servants of the vanquished god. These he placed under the charge of his father's own faithful chiefs, and made his father once more king over the lands from which he had been driven.

KAUILANI FINDS HIS SISTER LEPE-A-MOA

For some time after the famous battle with the evil god, Kauilani aided his parents in establishing a firm and peaceful government, after which he became restless and wanted new experiences.

One day he asked his mother if he was the only child she had. She told him the story of his sister, who had been born from an egg, and had become a very beautiful young woman. They had never seen her, because she had been taken to Oahu by her grandparents and there brought up.

Kauilani said, "I am going to Oahu to find her."

His mother said: "Yes, that is right. I will tell you about my people and their lands." So she told him about his ancestors, his grandparents and their rich lands around the Nuuanu stream and its bordering plains; also of the stopping-places as he should cross the island to Kapalama, his grandmother, where he would find his sister under a rainbow having certain strong shades of color.

The parents prepared a red feather cloak for him to wear with his fine magic malo. These he put on, and, taking his ancestral spear, went down to the sea. Laying his spear on the water, he poised upon it, when it dashed like a great fish through the water; leaping from wave to wave, it swept over the sea like a malolo (flying-fish), and landed him on the Oahu beach among the sand-dunes of Waianae.

Taking up his spear he started toward the sunrise side of the island, calling upon it as he went along to direct his path to Kapalama. Then he threw the spear as if it were a dart in the game of pahee, but instead of sliding and skipping along the ground it leaped into the air, and, like a bird floating on its wings, went along before the young chief.

Once it flew fast and far ahead of him to a place where two women were working, and fell at their feet. They saw the beautiful spear, wonderfully polished, and picked it up, and quickly found a hiding-place wherein they concealed it. Covering up the deep furrow it had made in the ground where it fell and looking around without seeing any one, they resumed their work.

Soon Kauilani came to the place where they were, and, greeting them, asked pleasantly, "When did you see my travelling companion who passed this way?" They were a little confused, yet said they had not seen any one.

Then he asked them plainly if a spear had passed them, and again they denied all knowledge of anything coming near. Kauilani said, "Have you not concealed my friend, my spear?"

They replied: "No. We have not had anything to do with any spear."

The chief softly called, "E Koa-wi! E Koa-wa! E!" The spear replied in a small, sharp voice, "E-o-e-o!" and leaped out from its hiding-place, knocking the women over into the stream near which they had been working.

Taking the spear, he went down to the seashore, scolding it on the way for making sport of him, and threatened to break it if anything else went wrong. The spear said: "You must not injure me, your ancestor, or all your visit will result in failure. But if you lay me down on the beach I will take you to the place where you can find your sister."

The chief said, "How shall I know you are not deceiving me?"

The spear replied, "Sit down on me and in a little while we shall be at a place where you can see her." Then it carried the complaining chief to the beach of Kou. There it lay on the ground and said: "You see a tree, a wiliwili-* tree, standing alone near the sea and looking out over the waters? Go you to that tree and climb it and look along the beach until you see a rainbow rising over the waves. Under that rainbow you will see a girl catching squid and shellfish and gathering sea-moss. She is doing this for her old people. She is your sister."

The chief said, "I will go and see, but if no one is there I will punish you for deceiving me, and break you into little pieces."

He went to the tree, climbed to the top branches and looked along the beach as the spear had directed. He saw a very strange thing out over the water: red mist and bloody rain-clouds moving back and forth over the dark-blue waves, extending far out toward the horizon and also covering the place where he was to see the girl. He called down to the spear that he could not see any rainbow or any girl.

The spear replied: "Everything is changing rapidly on the face of the sea. Look again."

* Erythrina Monosperma

222

He watched the whirling mist and rain, and as it moved slowly he saw an immense bird with many red feathers on its body and wings. When it flew up from the sea it hid the light from the sun and cast a dark shadow over all that beach.

He called to the spear, "What is this great bird flying over the ocean?"

The spear replied: "That is one of your ancestors, a kupua. She has a double body, sometimes appearing as a bird and sometimes in human form. Her name is Ka-iwa-ka-la-meha. She has dwelling-places in all the islands, and even in Kahiki. She has come to your sister, Lepe-a-moa, over the seas of the gods Ka-ne and Kanaloa."

Kauilani watched the great bird as it rose from the sea and flew in mighty circles around the heavens, rising higher and higher until it was lost in the sky.

Soon the atmosphere began to clear, and he saw the rainbow and the girl in the far distance. He came down and told the spear that all its words were true. The spear again asked the young chief to sit on it. He did so, and was carried rapidly to the group of houses where Kapalama was living with her husband and grandchild.

That same day, after Lepe-a-moa had taken her basket and gone to the shore, Kapalama looked along the road toward the sunset and saw a small cloud hastening along the way. Watching it carefully, she saw a rainbow in the cloud and called to her husband: "O Honouliuli, this is a very strange thing, but from the rainbow in the cloud I know that our grandchild from Kauai is coming to this place. You must quickly fire the oven and prepare food for this our young grandchild."

He made the oven ready, and soon had chicken, fish, and sweet-potatoes cooking for their visitor.

When Kauilani came to his grandparents they all wailed over each other, according to the ancient custom of the Hawaiians. When the greeting was finished he went into the house set apart for men as their eating-place, into which women were not allowed to enter, and there ate his food. After this he went outside and lay down on a mat and talked with his grandmother.

She praised him for the great victory won with his spear against his father's enemy, and then asked why he had come to Oahu.

He said, "I have come to see my sister in her double nature."

She replied: "That is right. I will take you to her house. There you must make a hollow place and hide under the mats and not let her see or hear you, lest you die. But when she falls asleep you must catch her and hold her fast until she accepts you as her brother. I will utter my chants and prayers for your success." So he hid himself in the girl's house and kept very quiet.

Meanwhile Lepe-a-moa, who was through fishing, picked up her basket and started toward her home. She saw a rainbow resting over their houses and thought some strange chief had come. She rejoiced and determined that the chief should play her favorite game konane, a game resembling checkers. When she came to the houses she asked her grandmother for the strange chief, saying she saw the footsteps of some man, perhaps now concealed by the grandmother.

Kapalama denied that any one had come. So the girl went into her house, laid aside her human body, and assumed that of many kinds of birds. Kapalama broke cooked sweet-potatoes and fed the pieces to this bird-body. Having eaten all she wished, Lepe-a-moa went into her house and lay down on her mats and fell asleep.

When deep sleep was on her the young chief leaped upon her, caught her in his arms, and held her fast. Jumping up, she dashed out of the house, carrying him with her. She flew up into the sky, but he still clung to her. The magic power of that spear helped him to hold fast and made the bird fly slowly.

As she heard her grandmother chanting about herself and her brother, the young chief of Kauai, her anger modified, and she asked the stranger, "Who are you, and from whence have you come?" He said, "I am from Kauai, and I am Kauilani, your younger brother."

Then she began to love him, and flew back to her grandparents, who welcomed them with great rejoicing.

For many days the young people and their grandparents dwelt happily together. In later years the young chief and his sister saved King Kakuhihewa in a remarkable manner. As a result, the king gave his favorite daughter to Kauilani as his wife, and Lepe-a-moa cared for their children.

THE BATTLE OF THE KUPUAS

This part of the legend of Lepe-a-moa belongs to Waikiki and to Palama.* It is also one of the ancient long stories handed down from generation to generation among the Hawaiians. It came from the days of Kakuhihewa, who was the King Arthur of Oahu traditions and whose chiefs were "the Knights of the Round Table" after whom most of the noted localities of Oahu were named. However, this goes back into the misty past only about four hundred years.

* A district in Chinatown, Honolulu.

A boy and a girl were born on the island of Kauai, both possessing miraculous powers. The girl, Lepe-a-moa, was taken as soon as born to Palama, and there brought up by her grandparents. The boy, Kauilani, was reared by his parents on Kauai, and there did many wonderful deeds, after which he came to Oahu to visit his sister.

At birth, Lepe-a-moa was only an egg, which, under the care of the grandparents, developed into a very beautiful maiden who could assume at will a multitude of bird forms. Thus she was what the ancient legends called kupua, or a person having both human and animal powers.

The young chief desired to visit the court of Kakuhihewa, who resided at Waikiki.* The grandmother, Kapalama, sent messengers to Ke-ao-lewa, the ruler of the birds of the heavens, for new clothing fit for the young chief, and they returned with a magnificent feather sash, and a glorious red feather cloak, shining like the blossoms of the lehua-tree, and fringed with yellow feathers which were like golden clouds in the light of the setting sun.

He bound the sash over his shoulders and around his body as a girdle, or malo, threw the cloak from the heavens around him, took his magic spear, Koa-wi Koa-wa, which had the

* Near Moana Hotel and Outrigger Club House.

227

power of human speech, and journeyed to Waikiki.

At this time Kakuhihewa was entertaining his sister and her husband, Maui-nui, who was king of the island of Maui. According to custom, the days were devoted to sports and gambling.

Maui-nui had a kupua, a rooster, which was one of the ancestors of Kauilani's family, but was very cruel and destructive. He could assume a different bird form for each magic power he possessed. This, with his miraculous human powers, made him superior to all the roosters which had ever been his antagonists in cock-fighting. It was the custom of this king to take this kupua in his rooster body, with some other chickens, and visit other chiefs, having many battles and winning large amounts of property, such as the best canoes, the finest mats and kapas, and the most royal feather cloaks, as well as the lands of the chiefs who had not been subject to him. Sometimes, when all available property had been won, he would persuade a chief to "bet his bones." This meant that the poverty-stricken chief, as a last resort, would wager his body against some of the property lost. If defeated, his life might be taken and his body sent to the most noted heiau (temple) of his opponent and placed on an altar as a human sacrifice, or the body would be burned or cooked in a fire oven and thrown into the sea.

Kakuhihewa and Maui-nui had been passing many days in this sport. When the Maui king was afraid the game might be given up, he would let some of the ordinary chickens fight, or would select the weakest from his flock. Then a large amount of property might be returned to the original owners, but he took care to lead his opponents on until their pride or their shame compelled them to wager their very last resources.

Thus the betting had gone on from time to time until the Maui king had provoked Kakuhihewa into betting his kingdom of Oahu in an almost hopeless attempt to win back all that had been lost before.

The Oahu king realized that his brother-in-law was using a bird of magic power, but his bets had been made and word given, and he did not know of any way in which he could get sufficient magic to overcome his antagonist. He had heard about Kauilani, a wonderfully powerful young chief on Kauai, who had conquered a god of the seas and restored a kingdom to his father. He had sent messengers to Kauai to ask this young chief to come to his aid, promising as a reward the hand of his favorite and most beautiful daughter in marriage; but the days passed and no word came from Kauai. Meanwhile Kauilani came before Kakuhihewa and was announced as a young chief from Kapalama. No one thought of any connection with the noted warrior of Kauai.

The king was very much pleased with the young chief, and finally asked him if he had seen his chickens, and if he would like to go to the place where they were kept.

Kauilani saw the chickens and sent for water, which the keepers brought to him. Taking it, he sprinkled the eyes of the roosters. None of them had sufficient power to keep from shutting their eyes when the water struck their heads. Then he said to the keeper, "These birds will not be of any use for our chief."

Then he went to see the king's tabu rooster, the one reserved by the king for any last and desperate conflict. This he also tried and found wanting.

The keepers then sent word to the king that a strange young man with great wisdom was looking at the chickens, and the king came out and asked Kauilani about the tests.

The young chief sprinkled water as before, and then said to the king, "Perhaps your rooster has strength and perhaps he has no power."

The king said: "Ah! We see that this tabu rooster has no strength for this conflict. He closes his eyes. His enemy is very strong and very quick. We shall be defeated and belong to the king of Maui."

Then Kauilani said, "Perhaps I can find a bird of very great powers who can save us."

The king said: "If you defeat Ke-au-hele-moa, the magic rooster of the king of Maui, you shall become my son. My daughter shall be your wife."

Kauilani requested the king to have the place closed where the chickens were kept, so that no spy could watch them. He told the king he had a kupua chicken still in an egg, which would kill the great bird of the king of Maui, but that before the time came for the festival in which the cock-fighting occurred his chicken would be hatched and have power to save the king and his kingdom. The king was filled with delight, and took the handsome young chief at once to his house and sent for his daughter.

He said to her: "I have set you free from the tabu which I placed upon you as the promised wife of the chief of Kauai. It is better that you should take this young chief as your husband."

So they were married and lived together a few days. Then the young chief told the king he must go at once to obtain the chicken egg. He told his wife not to be jealous about anything she might hear among the people, and not to be angry in any way whatever at the time of his return, or he would not continue to have her as his wife.

He went back to his sister, Lepe-a-moa. She saw him, and leaped to meet him, calling: "Come! Come! Come! I have waited and waited for you."

He told her all about his visit and the great need of the king, saying, "I have come back for this day only and for your help."

Then they went to the bathing-pool, and were swimming, diving and bathing when they heard the sweet voice of the mischievous elepaio bird over them, around them, and at last from the bank of the pool, calling out: "Ono ka ia! Ono ka ia!" ("The fish is sweet! The fish is sweet!") This bird was also Lea, the goddess of canoe-cutters.

Kauilani called to her: "Why do you not get young fish in the ocean? Is this the only place for sweet fish?"

Then the elepaio told the brother and sister about the great rooster belonging to the king of Maui, its miraculous power, and its name, "Ke-au-hele-moa," and then said:

"You two go to the place of the fight. Take great care of your sister. Put her in a lei garland around your neck. You will note the appearance of that rooster of the king of Maui: very tall; black, white and red feathers; only one tail-feather. If he sees his grandchild before the fight she will not escape, but if you keep her hidden until she goes out for battle he will be destroyed."

When the brother and sister returned they told the grandparents about Kakuhihewa's trouble and the power of the rooster of the king of Maui to assume several bodies. Kauilani told them that the Maui king was so sure of winning that he had collected a great pile of wood wherewith to heat an oven in which to cook Kakuhihewa's body.

The grandmother said: "That great bird is one of our own family, and has very great power, but Lepe-a-moa has much greater power if you two work together. He must not see her until she goes out to fight with him."

Lepe-a-moa said to her brother: "This is bad for you. You come as if you loved me, but you have taken the king's daughter for your wife. If I go with you and your wife is angry with me, she shall be set aside and I will be your wife." Kauilani said, "That is right."

Lepe-a-moa made herself very beautiful with a glistening spotted feather cloak. Her pa-u, or skirt, was like fire, flaming and flashing. Kauilani told her she must go first, as the eldest one of the family. Thus they passed in their splendid feather dresses down to Kou (Honolulu) and out to Pawaa, the people shouting and praising the beautiful girl.

As they came to Waikiki the noise of the people could be heard far, far away: "O the beautiful girl coming with the husband of our chiefess! O the beautiful girl!"

The king's daughter heard the shout and became very angry. She ordered the people to drive Kauilani and Lepe-a-moa away.

But the servants knew the reason why the young chief had become the husband of the king's daughter, and said among themselves: "We want to live. We must not drive them away."

Lepe-a-moa said to her brother, "I told you that she would be angry with me."

"Yes," said the brother, "that is true, and you shall be my wife."

They turned aside from the royal houses. The girl laid aside her gift body and put on her bird body in one of its smallest forms and was concealed in an egg. The brother wrapped this egg in a corner of his cloak, put it around his neck and went to the place where the chickens were kept and took one of the small houses of the keepers as his own.

That evening, when a large calabash of food was brought for the chickens and set aside, he took it secretly, gave all the food to his sister and turned the calabash up as if it had been upset and the food eaten by dogs. The caretakers were greatly worried because they had no food that night for the chickens. They knew that the chickens would not have any strength for fighting.

When Kakuhihewa heard that his daughter had driven her husband away he was very much troubled, and was afraid that he and his people would be destroyed, so he sent messengers to look everywhere and if possible find the young chief, but they all failed.

At last one of the guardians of the chickens said, "Your son is sleeping in one of our houses."

Kakuhihewa sent Kou, one of the highest officers in his government, to go after Kauilani. This Kou was the chief after whom Kou, the ancient Honolulu, was named. Kou found the young chief sleeping, and aroused him, telling him the king was very sorry for the anger of his daughter, and asking him to come back to the king's house and on the morrow see the day of death.

Kauilani told Kou to return and tell the king to prepare everything for the day of battle, and hang a large kapa sheet between two posts. He pointed out two roosters which were to be taken first. The king was to send them one by one to fight. When they were killed the king was to ask for a time of rest. "After this will be the time for my battle." Thus he taught Kou, who returned and told the king.

The next morning the king of Maui sent his messenger to the king of Oahu, asking if all things were ready for the battle of that day.

The king of Oahu replied: "Yes; we will go to the place of death. If they win, we die; but if we win, there shall be no death. I do not know how to kill a man in this way."

So they all went to the battlefield. As soon as all the chiefs and the people were assembled, Maui-nui, king of Maui, leaped up and began his boast, proposing the battle and stating the conditions, "Death for the defeated." Kakuhihewa quietly answered: "If I win, I shall not kill you. You have already prepared for our death."

The wife of the king of Maui favored the terms of the Oahuan ruler to be applied to both sides, but her husband again called out his condition, "Death to the defeated."

Then Kakuhihewa stated his condition: "We will try one rooster, and then another. If both of my roosters are killed, we will rest until time has been given to get another bird for me."

This was agreed to without any opposition.

The chickens were quickly freed. The roosters leaped against each other and one fell dead. Then the second battle was fought and the second rooster killed.

While they were resting, Kauilani went in behind that large kapa sheet which he had

requested. The egg was wrapped in his cloak,
which was thrown around his neck. He took out
the egg and uttered an incantation:

> "The chicken comes out better in the heat.
> Both of us were born at midnight.
> Dust rises and is blown like mist on a wave.
> Pick the flowers of the ohia—pick the flowers.
> Fly! Fly! Fly!
> Leaping in the dust of Kaumaea."

The egg began to change until it became a
full-grown chicken.

Kauilani told his bird-sister to go out before
the people thus: "Go all around the fighting-
place. Go to the feet of Maui-nui, and look upon
him; then go to the middle and stand there looking into the face of your ancestor. He will then
know you perhaps, and will put on many kinds of
bird bodies. If he puts on red, you must become
white. You have more bird bodies than he. You
will win. Then if he changes his body again I will
tell you what to do until he becomes weary; then
you put on your spotted body and kill him."

The bird then left him and went out before
the people. They made a great noise, laughing
and crying out: "A hen! A hen! To fight the great
rooster!"

But she was very beautiful in her shining coat
of feathers as she waited for the battle. Then the

rooster came in, and Kauilani saw that he did not recognize his grandchild. Lepe-a-moa clucked and moved her head and wings like a hen calling to her young chickens. Ke-au-hele-moa was angry. His feathers rose as he came up and he changed their color into red. His antagonist became white.

Then he struck at her, leaped at her, and tried to overthrow her with his wings, but was not able to touch her, while she lightly flew over his head, striking his face and beating him with claws and wings.

Then he became moa-nene (a goose form), but Kauilani uttered a prayer and his sister became a swift aloe-bird, a small mud-hen. The battle again was fought, whirling, striking, leaping and flying, but the bird-girl was not injured in the least, while the rooster's face was bleeding and his eyes suffering from the terrific and swift blows dealt by Lepe-a-moa. She tore him to pieces, until the battle was in a thick cloud of flying feathers.

The people thought he was dead, but his magic power was still in the fragments of his body, torn and thrown up, floating far up among the clouds. He rested in some mist-clouds above, and put on a body having the color of the yellow blossoms of the hau-tree.

Before this the day had been quiet, but now, with the return of that rooster, the chill of snow

and ice came down in a cold mist like the snow
mists on the tops of the mountains. The rooster
sent this icy, fine rain in a stream like a flowing
river over Kakuhihewa and his people.

Then Kauilani called to his sister: "Behold
Ke-au-hele-moa comes to his last strength. He
follows the ice-cloud. Can you make a way of
escape?" This call was in a spirit voice and none
of the people heard.

Lepe-a-moa called upon Ke-ao-lewa (The
morning cloud) for help, and a cloud was let
down as a shield, turning off the cold mist and
letting it pass on over the sea. So Kakuhihewa
and his people were left in peace.

Lepe-a-moa flew up into a tall coconut-tree
and saw her enemy in the form of a manu-alala
(great black bird) coming behind the mist to the
battlefield. She flew down and put on the color
of the pua-niu (the cream color of a coconut
blossom) and again flew like a whirlwind
around her enemy. Then the ancestor-bird took
his last body, that of a moa-a-uha.

Kauilani called to his sister to go around
before all the people, putting on her spotted
body, and then return, looking sharply at the
right wing of her enemy to find a place to break
it, then fly against the right eye and pick it out,
and after that fly down on the head of the king
of Maui, then leap to the last battle, break the

left wing, pluck out the left eye and tear the body to pieces. "Then he will die. He cannot make a new body for himself."

Lepe-a-moa flew down upon the black bird, which tried to strike her with its strong wings, but when the right wing was spread out, showing its weak places, she flew in swiftly and broke that wing so that it could not be used. Then she leaped against the head and caught the right eye, destroying it. The black bird tried to whirl around and around to strike the spotted chicken, but Lepe-a-moa shook her wings over her enemy and flew off around the place of battle until she was in front of the Maui king. Before he could think or make a move for self-protection she dashed into his hair and tore it with her claws and flew back against her enemy. This polluted and disgraced Maui-nui.

This time she whirled around the left side. He struck at her. As his wing was spread out she flew in and broke it, so that it fell useless by his side. Then she struck his eye, and he was entirely blind. She dashed against him, and he fell over. She clawed and picked and tore his body until it was in small pieces and his life was destroyed.

The people shouted with a loud voice: "Auwe! Auwe! [Alas! Alas!] The rooster of the king of Maui is dead! Ke-au-hele-moa is dead! The king of Maui is to die!"

The name of this rooster, it is said, was given to a place far up Palolo Valley, near Honolulu.

When the people shouted, Kauilani stood up in his splendid cloak and sash and cried out: "Aye! Aye! Dead to me—dead to Kauilani, the child of Keahua and Kauhao!"

His sister flew to him and he took her and disappeared in the confused, moving crowd of excited people. Thus they returned to Kapalama.

At that time Kakuhihewa learned who the young man was, and was glad that he had not treated him uncivilly in any way and so lost his wonderful aid. He was very, very thankful for his victory over the king of Maui

He ordered his servants to find Kauilani, but they could not. He was fully lost.

Wailuku, the wife of Maui-nui, asked Kakuhihewa what he intended to do with them.

He replied: "I will not kill. I am for life. I do not know how to make a man. I do not want death. If you had won, you should have your desire. Now I will have life as my wish."

Maui-nui returned to his island, but his wife remained with her brother.

The king ordered his people to make search everywhere for Kauilani. They went to Kauai, but he had not returned to his parents. They visited Maui and Hawaii, but found no trace. For several months the search was prosecuted.

Even the mountains, hills, valleys, forests, jungles and caves were looked over as carefully as possible. By and by two chiefs, Kou and Waikiki, saw the signs of a high chief over Kapalama's group of houses, and went up to make inquiries. They saw Kauilani and told him that the king wanted him to come back.

Lepe-a-moa said: "You must reveal yourself, and you must go back to that wife. Her time has come."

Kauilani sent the chiefs, Kou and Waikiki, back to the king with the message that he would follow the next day.

In the morning he met the king, who said: "This year I have been near to death and from you came life, and you have been lost, to my sorrow. Now my daughter's child is near birth, perhaps you can give life to your child."

Kauilani went to his wife's home. The caretakers refused to let him give any aid until they had tried all their arts and failed.

Then Kauilani sent all the people away and stood alone by his wife, uttering his chant or incantation of life for the sick one:

"O Aumakuas! Ghost gods!
    Come from the north, the south, the east, the west.
    Male and female and children,
    Come for this cry of distress.

O all those who have power in the skies!
Come in this time of death.
O all the household of Kapalama!
Come and give life.
I am Kauilani,
The strong child of Keahua and Kauhao.
Life for the mother and this child."

While he was chanting this prayer the child was born. Lepe-a-moa saw that her brother was very busy before the gods, so she secretly took the child and hurried to Kapalama.

That day there were fierce storms, resounding thunder and flashing lightning, while the land shook in the throes of an earthquake. These were the signs usually accompanying the birth of any high chief or chiefess.

Kakuhihewa was troubled when he knew that the child had disappeared, but was satisfied when he learned that it was with Kapalama and Lepe-a-moa.

The baby was a girl and very beautiful, so Lepe-a-moa adopted it as her own and gave it the name of Kamamo.

Kauilani lived with his wife, making his home all the rest of his life in the court of his father-in-law, Kakuhihewa.

Chapter 25

KAMAPUAA LEGENDS

LEGENDS OF THE HOG-GOD

Some of the most unique legends of the nations have centered around imagined monsters. Centaurs, half man and half horse, thronged the dreams of Rome. The Hawaiians knew nothing about any animals save the fish of the seas, the birds of the forests, and the chickens, the dogs and the pigs around their homes. From the devouring shark the Hawaiian imagination conceived the idea of the shark-man who indulged in cannibalistic tendencies. From the devastations of the hogs they built up the experiences of an rude vicious chief whom they called Kamapuaa, who was the principal figure of many rough exploits throughout the islands. Sometimes he had a hog's body with a human head and limbs, sometimes a hog's head rested on a human form, and sometimes he assumed the shape of a hog—quickly reassuming the form of a man. Kalakaua's legends say that he was a hairy man and cultivated the stiff hair by cutting it short so that it stood out like bristles, and that he had his body tattooed so that it would have the appearance of a hog. In place of the ordinary feather cloak worn by chiefs he wore a pigskin with its bristles on the outside and a pigskin girdle around his waist.

The legends say that he was born at Kaluanui, a part of the district of Hauula or Koolau coast of the island Oahu. His reputed father was Olopana, the high chief of that part of the island, and his mother was Hina, the daughter of a chief who had come from a foreign land. Other legends say that his father was Kahikiula (The Red Tahiti), a brother of Olopana. These brothers had come to Oahu from foreign lands some time before. Fornander always speaks of Olopana as Kamapuaa's uncle, although he had taken Hina as his wife.

The Koolauloa coast of Oahu lies as a luxuriant belt of ever-living foliage a mile or so in width between an ocean of many colors and dark beetling precipices of mountain walls rising some thousands of feet among the clouds.

From these precipices which mark the landward side of a mighty extinct crater come many mountain streams leaping in cascades of spray down into the quiet green valleys which quickly broaden into the coral-reef-bordered seacoast. From any place by the sea the outline of several beautiful little valleys can be easily traced.

One morning while the sunlight of May looked into the hidden recesses and crevices of these valleys, bringing into sharp relief of shadow and light the outcropping ledges, a little band of Hawaiians and their white friends lay in the shade of a great kamani* tree and talked about the legends which were told of the rugged rock masses of each valley, and the quiet pools of each rivulet. Where the little party lay was one of the sporting-places of Kamapuaa the "hog-child treated in the legends as a demigod." Not far away one of the mountain streams had broadened into a quiet bush-shaded lakelet with deep fringes of grass around its borders. Here the legendary hog-man with marvellous powers had bathed from time to time. A narrow gorge deep shadowed by the morning sun was the place which Kamapuaa had miraculously bridged for his followers when an enemy was closely pursuing them. Several large stones on the edges of the valleys were pointed out as the monuments of various adventures. An exquisitely formed little valley ran deep into the mountain almost in front of the legend-tellers. Far away in the upper end where the dark-green foliage blended with still darker shadows the sides of the valley narrowed until they were only from sixty to seventy feet apart, and

* Calophyllum Inophyllum.

unscalable precipices bent toward each other,
leaving only a narrow strip of sky above. On the
right of this valley is a branch-gorge down
which fierce storms have hurled torrents of
waters and mist. The upper end has been hollowed and polished in the shape of a finely
rounded canoe of immense proportions. It was
from this that the valley took its name Ka-liu-
waa, possibly having the meaning, "the leaky
canoe." Some of the legends say that this was
Kamapuaa's canoe leaning against the precipice
and always leaking out the waters which fell in
it. Lying toward the west was a very fertile and
open tract of land, Kaluanui, where Kamapuaa
was said to have been born of Hina. After his
birth he was thrown away by Kahiki-houna-
kele, an older brother, and left to die. After a
time Hina, the mother, went to a stream of clear,
sweet water near her home to bathe. After
bathing she went to the place where she had left
her pa-u, or tapa skirt, and found a fine little
hog lying on it. She picked it up and found that
it was a baby. She was greatly alarmed, and gave
the hog-child to another son, Kekelaiaika, that
he might care for it, but the older brother stole
the hog-child and carried it away to a cave in
which Hina's mother lived. Her name was
Kamaunuaniho. The grandmother knew the
hog-child at once as her grandson endowed with

marvellous powers, and since the gods had
given him the form of a hog he should be called
kama (child), puaa (hog). Then she gave to the
older brother kapa quilts in which to place
Kamapuaa. These were made in layers, six
sheets of kapa cloth formed the under quilt for
a bed and six sheets the upper quilt for a cover.
In these Kamapuaa slept while his brother prepared taro* and breadfruit for his food. Thus
the wonderful hog ate and slept usually in the
form of a hog until size and strength came to
him. Then he became mischievous and began to
commit depredations at night. He would root
up the taro in the fields of his neighbors, and
especially in the field of the high chief Olopana.
Then he would carry the taro home, root up
ferns and grass until he had good land and then
plant the stolen taro. Thus his grandmother and
her retainers were provided with growing taro,
the source of which they did not understand.

His elder brother prepared an oven in which
to cook chickens. Kamapuaa rooted up the oven
and stole the chickens. This brother Kahiki-
houna-kele caught the hog-child and adminis-
tered a sound whipping, advising him to go
away from home if he wanted to steal, and especially to take what he wanted from Olopana.
Adopting this advice, Kamapuaa extended his

* Calocasia antiquorum.

raids to the home of the high chief. Here he found many chickens. Kamapuaa quickly killed some, took them in his mouth and threw many more on his back and ran home. The morning came before he had gone far and the people along the way saw the strange sight and pursued him. By the use of charms taught him by his sorceress° grandmother he made himself run faster and faster until he had outstripped his pursuer. Then he carried his load to his grandmother's cave and gave the chickens to the family for a great luau (feast).

Another time he stole the sacred rooster belonging to Olopana, as well as many other fowls. The chief sent a large number of warriors after him. They chased the man who had been seen carrying the chickens. He fled by his grandmother's cave and threw the chickens inside, then fled back up the hillside, revealing himself to his pursuers. They watched him, but he disappeared. He dropped down by the side of a large stone. On this he seated himself and watched the people as they ran through the valley calling to each other. The high grass was around the stone so that for a long time he was concealed. For this reason this stone still bears the name Pohaku-pee-o-Kamapuaa (Kamapuaa's-hiding-stone). After a time a man who had climbed to the opposite ridge cried out, "E, E, there he is sitting on the great stone!" This man was turned into a stone by the magic of Kamapuaa. The pursuers hastened up the hillside and surrounded the stone, but no man was there. There was a fine black hog, which they recognized as the wonderful one belonging to Kamaunuaniho. So they decided that this was the thief, and seized it and carried it down the hill to give to the high chief Olopana. After getting him down into the valley they tried to drive him, but he would not go. Then they sent into the forest for ohia poles and made a large litter. It required many men to carry this enormous hog, who made himself very heavy.

Suddenly Kamapuaa heard his grandmother calling: "Break the cords! Break the poles! Break the strong men! Escape!" Making a sudden turn on the litter, he broke it in pieces and fell with it to the ground. Then he burst the cords which bound him and attacked the band of men whom he had permitted to capture him. Some legends say that he killed and ate many of them. Others say that he killed and tore the people.

The wild life lived by Kamapuaa induced a large band of rough lawless men to leave the service of the various high chiefs and follow Kamapuaa in his marauding expeditions. They made themselves the terror of the whole Koolau region.

Olopana determined to destroy them, and sent an army of four hundred warriors to uproot Kamapuaa and his robbers. It was necessary for them to hasten to their hiding-places, but they were chased up into the hills until a deep gorge faced them. No way of escape seemed possible, but Kamapuaa, falling on the ground, became a long hog—stretching out he increased his length until he could reach from side to side of the deep ravine—thus he formed a bridge over which his followers escaped.

Kamapuaa, however, was not able to make himself small quickly enough to escape from his enemies. He tried to hide himself in a hole and pull dead branches and leaves over himself; but they soon found him, bound him securely, and tied him to a great stone which with "the stone of hiding" and "the watcher" are monuments of the legends to this day.

The people succeeded in leading the hog-man to Olopana's home, where they fastened him, keeping him for a great feast, which they hoped to have in a few days, but Kamapuaa, Samson-like, broke all his bonds, destroyed many of his captors—wantonly destroyed coconut-trees and taro patches, and then went back to his home.

He knew that Olopana would use every endeavor to compass his destruction. So he called his followers together and led them up Kaliuwaa Valley, stopping to get his grandmother on the way. When he came to the end of the valley, and the steep cliffs up which his people could not possibly climb, he took his grandmother on his neck and leaned back against the great precipice. Stretching himself more and more, and rubbing against the black rocks, at last he lifted his grandmother to the top of the cliffs so that she could step off on the uplands which sloped down to the Pearl Harbor side of the island. Then the servants and followers climbed up the sides of the great hog by clinging to his bristles and escaped. The hollow worn in the rocks looked like a hewn-out canoe, and was given the name Ka-waa-o-Kamapuaa (The canoe of Kamapuaa). Kamapuaa then dammed up the water of the beautiful stream by throwing his body across it, and awaited the coming of Olopana and his warriors.

An immense force had been sent out to destroy him. In addition to the warriors who came by land, a great fleet of canoes was sent along the seashore to capture any boats in which Kama-puaa and his people might try to escape.

The canoes gathered in and around the mouth of the stream which flowed from Kaliuwaa Valley. The warriors began to march along the stream up toward the deep gorge.

Suddenly Kamapuaa broke the dam by leaping away from the waters, and a great flood drowned the warriors, and dashed the canoes together, destroying many and driving the rest far out to sea. Uhakohi is said to be the place where this flood occurred.

Then Kamapuaa permitted the people to capture him. They went up the valley after the waters had subsided and found nothing left of Kamapuaa or his people except a small black hog. They searched the valley thoroughly. They found the canoe, turned to stone, leaning against the precipice at the end of the gorge. They said among themselves, "Escaped is Kamapuaa with all his people, and ended are our troubles."

They caught the hog and bound it to carry to Olopana. As they journeyed along the seashore their burden became marvellously heavy until at last an immense litter was required resting on the shoulders of many men. It was said that he sometimes tossed himself over to one side, breaking it down and killing some of the men who carried him. Then again he rolled to the other side, bringing a like destruction. Thus he brought trouble and death and a long, weary journey to his captors, who soon learned that their captive was the hog-man Kamapuaa. They brought him to their king Olopana and placed him in the temple enclosure where sacrifices to the gods were confined. This heiau was in Kaneohe and was known as the heiau of Kawaewae. It was in the care of a priest known as Lonoaohi.

Long, long before this capture Olopana had discovered Kamapuaa and would not acknowledge him as his son. The destruction of his coconut-trees and taro patches had been the cause of the first violent rupture between the two. Kamapuaa had wantonly broken the walls of Olopana's great fish-pond and set the fish free, and then after three times raiding the fowls around the grass houses had seized, killed and eaten the sacred rooster which Olopana considered his household fetish.

When Olopana knew that Kamapuaa had been captured and was lying bound in the temple enclosure he sent orders that great care should be taken lest he escape, and later he should be placed on the altar of sacrifice before the great gods.

Hina, it was said, could not bear the thought that this child of hers, brutal and injurious as he was, should suffer as a sacrifice. She was a very high chiefess, and, like the Hinas throughout Polynesia, was credited with divine powers. She had great influence with the high priest Lonoaohi and persuaded him to give Kamapuaa an opportunity to escape. This was done by killing a black hog and smearing Kamapuaa's body with the blood. Thus bearing the appearance of death, he was laid unbound on the altar. It was certain that unless detected he could easily climb the temple wall and escape.

Olopana, the king, came to offer the chants and prayers which belonged to such a sacrifice. He as well as the high priest had temple duties, and the privilege of serving at sacrifices of great importance. As was his custom he came from the altar repeating chants and prayers while Kamapuaa lay before the images of the gods. While he was performing the sacrificial rites, Kamapuaa became angry, leaped from the altar, changed himself into his own form, seized the bone daggers used in dismembering the sacrifices, and attacked Olopana, striking him again and again, until he dropped on the floor of the temple dead. The horrified priests had been powerless to prevent the deed, nor did they think of striking Kamapuaa down at once. In the confusion he rushed from the temple, fled along the coast to his well-known valleys, climbed the steep precipices and rejoined his grandmother and his followers.

Leading his band of rough robbers down through the sandalwood* forests of the Wahiawa region, he crossed over the plains to

* Illahi or Santalum.

the Waianae Mountains. Here they settled for a time, living in caves. Other lawless spirits joined them, and they passed along the Ewa side of the island, ravaging the land like a herd of swine. A part of the island they conquered, making the inhabitants their serfs.

Here on a spur of the Waianae Mountains they built a residence for Kama-unu-aniho, and established her as their priestess, or kahuna. They levied on the neighboring farmers for whatever taro, sweet-potatoes* and bananas they needed. They compelled the fishermen to bring tribute from the sea. They surrounded their homes with pigs and chickens, and in mere wantonness terrorized that part of Oahu.

KAMAPUAA ON OAHU AND KAUAI

Fornander says that Kamapuaa was sometimes called "the eight-eyed" and was also gifted with eight feet. He says, "This specialty of four faces or heads and of corresponding limbs is peculiar to some of the principal Hindoo deities." The honorary designation of gods and even high chiefs in Hawaiian mythology was frequently maka-walu (eight-eyed), to express their great endowment of divine powers. Fornander notes

* Ipomea Batatas.

"coincidence as bearing upon the derivation of Polynesian myths and legends. The Kamapuaa stories, however, seem to have no counterpart in any mythology beyond the borders of the Hawaiian Islands."

While he lived on the Koolau coast he was simply a devastating, brutal monster, with certain powers belonging to a demi-god, which he used as maliciously as possible. After being driven out to the Honolulu side of the mountains, for a time he led his band of robbers in their various expeditions, but after a time his miraculous powers increased and he went forth terrorizing the island from one end to the other. He had the power of changing himself into any kind of a fish. As a shark and as a hog he was represented as sometimes eating those whom he conquered in battle. He ravaged the fields and chicken preserves of the different chiefs, but it is said never stole or ate pigs or fish.

He wandered along the low lands from the taro patches of Ewa to the coconut groves of Waikiki, rooting up and destroying the food of the people.

At Kamoiliili he saw two beautiful women coming from the stream which flows from Manoa Valley. He called to them, but when they saw his tattooed body and rough clothing made from pigskins they recognized him and fled. He

257

pursued them, but they were counted as goddesses, having come from divine foreign families as well as Kamapuaa. They possessed miraculous powers and vanished when he was ready to place his hands upon them. They sank down into the earth. Kamapuaa changed himself into the form of a great hog and began to root up the stones and soil and break his way through the thick layer of petrified coral through which they had disappeared. He first followed the descent of the woman who had been nearest to him. Down he went through soil and stone after her, but suddenly a great flood of water burst upward through the coral almost drowning him. The goddess had stopped his pursuit by turning an underground stream into the entrance which he had made.*

After this narrow escape Kamapuaa rushed toward Manoa Valley to the place where he had seen the other beautiful woman disappear. Here also he rooted deep through earth and coral, and here again a new spring of living water was uncovered. He could do nothing against the flood, which threatened his life. The goddesses escaped and the two wells have supplied the people of Kamoiliili for many generations, bearing the name, "The wells, or fountains, of Kamapuaa."

* Near the Kamoiliili church.

The chief of Waikiki had a fine tract* well supplied with bananas and coconuts and taro. Night after night a great black hog rushed through Waikiki destroying all the ripening fruit and even going to the very doors of the grass houses searching out the calabashes filled with poi waiting for fermentation. These calabashes he dashed to the ground, defiling their contents and breaking and unfitting them for further use. A crowd of warriors rushed out to kill this devastating monster. They struck him with clubs and hurled their spears against his bristling sides. The stiff bristles deadened the force of the blows of the clubs and turned the spear-points aside so that he received but little injury. Meanwhile his fierce tusks were destroying the warriors and his cruel jaws were tearing their flesh and breaking their bones. In a short time the few who were able to escape fled from him. The chiefs gathered their warriors again and again, and after many battles drove Kamapuaa from cave to cave and from district to district. Finally he leaped into the sea, changed himself into the form of a fish and passed over the channel to Kauai.

He swam westward along the coast, selecting a convenient place for landing, and when night came, sending the people to their sleep, he went ashore. He had marked the location of taro and

* Near the Cleghorn residence.

sugar-cane patches and could easily find them in the night. Changing himself into a black hog he devoured and trampled the sugar-cane, rooted up taro and upset calabashes, eating the poi and breaking the wooden bowls. Then he fled to a rough piece of land which he had decided upon as his hiding-place.

The people were astonished at the devastation when they came from their houses next morning. Only gods who were angry could have wrought such havoc so unexpectedly, therefore they sent sacrifices to the heiaus, that the gods of their homes might protect them. But the next night other fields were made desolate as if a herd of swine had been wantonly at work all through the night. After a time watchmen were set around the fields and the mighty hog was seen. The people were called. They surrounded Kamapuaa, caught him and tied him with strongest cords of olona* fibre and pulled him to one side, that on the new day so soon to dawn they might build their oven and roast him for a great feast.

When they thought all was finished the hog suddenly burst his bonds, became invisible and leaped upon them, tore them and killed them as he had done on Oahu, then rushed away in the darkness.

Again some watchers found him lying at the foot of a steep precipice, sleeping in the day-

* Touchardia latifolia.

time. On the edge of the precipice were great boulders, which they rolled down upon him, but he was said to have allowed the stones to strike him and fall shattered in pieces while he sustained very little injury.

Then he assumed the form of a man and made his home by a ledge of rock called Kipukai. Here there was a spring of very sweet water, which lay in the form of a placid pool of clear depths, reflecting wonderfully whatever shadows fell upon its surface. To this two beautiful sisters were in the habit of coming with their water-calabashes. While they stooped over the water Kamapuaa came near and cast the shadow as a man before them on the clear waters. They both wanted the man as their husband who could cast such a shadow. He revealed himself to them and took them both to be his wives. They lived with him at Kipukai and made fine sleeping mats for him, cultivated food and prepared it for him to eat. They pounded kapa that he might be well clothed.

At that time there were factions on the island of Kauai warring against each other. Fierce hand-to-hand battles were waged and rich spoils carried away.

With the coming of Kamapuaa to Kauai a new and strange appearance wrought terror in the hearts of the warriors whenever a battle occurred. While the conflict was going on and blows were freely given by both club and spear, suddenly a massive war-club would be seen whistling through the air, striking down the chiefs of both parties. Mighty blows were struck by this mysterious club. No hand could be seen holding it, no strong arm swinging it, and no chief near it save those stricken by it. Dead and dying warriors covered the ground in its path. Sometimes when Kamapuaa had been caught in his marauding expedition, he would escape from the ropes tying him, change into a man, seize a club, become invisible and destroy his captors. He took from the fallen their rich feather war cloaks, carried them to his dwelling-place and concealed them under his mats. The people of Kauai were terrified by the marvellous and powerful being who dwelt in their midst. They believed in the ability of kahunas, or priests, to work all manner of evil in strange ways and therefore were sure that some priest was working with evil spirits to compass their destruction. They sought the strongest and most sacred of their own kahunas, but were unable to conquer the evil. Meanwhile Kamapuaa, tired of the two wives, began to make life miserable for them, trying to make them angry, that he might have good excuse for killing them. They knew something of his mar-

vellous powers as a demi-god, and watched him
when he brought bundles to his house and put
them away. The chief's house then as in later
years was separated from the houses of the
women and was tabu to them, but they waited
until they had seen him go far away. Then they
searched his house and found the war cloaks of
their friends under his mats. They hastened and
told their friends, who plotted to take
vengeance on their enemy.

The women decided to try to drive the
demigod away, so destroyed the spring of water
from which they had daily brought water for his
need. They also carefully concealed all evidences of other springs. Kamapuaa returned
from his adventures and was angry when he
found no water waiting for him. He called for
the women, but they had hidden themselves. He
was very thirsty. He rushed to the place of the
spring, but could not find it. He looked for
water here and there, but the sisters had woven
mighty spells over all the water-holes and he
could not see them. In his rage he rushed about
like a blind and crazy man. Then the sisters
appeared and ridiculed him. They taunted him
with his failure to overcome their wiles. They
laughed at his suffering. Then in his great anger
he leaped upon them, caught them and threw
them over a precipice. As they fell upon the

ground he uttered his powerful incantations and changed them into two stones, which for many generations have been guardians of that precipice. Then he assumed the form of a hog and rooted deep in the rocky soil. Soon he uncovered a fountain of water from which he drank deeply, but which he later made bitter and left as a mineral-spring to the present day.

The people of Kauai now knew the secret of the wonderful swinging war club. They knew that a hand held it and an invisible man walked beside it, so they fought against a power which they could not see. They felt their clubs strike some solid body even when they struck at the air. Courage came back to them, and at Hanalei the people forced him into a corner, and, carrying stones, tried to fence him in, but he broke the walls down, tore his way through the people and fled. The high chief of Hanalei threw his magic spear at him as he rushed past, but missed him. The spear struck the mountainside near the summit and passed through, leaving a great hole through which the sky on the other side of the mountain can still be seen. Kamapuaa decided that he was tired of Kauai, therefore he ran to the seashore, leaped into the water and, becoming a fish, swam away to Hawaii.

PELE AND KAMAPUAA

The three great mountains of Hawaii had been built many centuries before Pele found an abiding home in the pit of Kilauea. Kilauea itself appears rather as a shelter to which she fled than as a house of her own building. The sea waters quenched the fires built by her at lower levels, forcing her up higher and higher toward the mountains until she took refuge in the maelstrom of eternal fire known for centuries among the Hawaiians as Ka lua o Pele (The pit of Pele),—the boiling centre of the active pit of fire. Some legends say that Kamapuaa drove Pele from place to place by pouring in water.

The Kalakaua legends probably give the correct idea of the growths of Pele-worship as the goddess of volcanic fires when they say that the Pele family of brave and venturesome high chiefs with their followers settled under the shadows of the smoke-clouds from Kilauea and were finally destroyed by some overwhelming eruption. And yet the destruction was so spectacular, or at least so mysterious, that the idea took firm root that Pele and her brothers and sisters, instead of passing out of existence, entered into the volcano to dwell there as living spirits having the fires of the under-world as their continual heritage. From this home of fire

Pele and her sisters could come forth assuming the forms in which they had been seen as human beings. This power has been the cause of many legends about Pele and her adventures with various chiefs whom she at last overwhelmed with boiling floods of lava tossed out of her angry heart. In this way she appeared in different parts of the island of Hawaii apparently no longer having any fear of danger to her home from incoming seas.

The last great battle between sea and fire was connected with Pele as a fire-goddess and Kamapuaa, the demi-god, part hog and part man. It is a curious legend in which human and divine elements mingle like the changing scenes of a dream. This naturally follows the statement in some of the legends that Ku, one of the highest gods among the Polynesians as well as among the Hawaiians, was an ancestor of Kamapuaa, protecting him and giving him the traits of a demi-god. Kamapuaa had passed through many adventures on the islands of Oahu and Kanai, and had lived for a time on Maui. He had, according to some of the legends, developed his mysterious powers so that he could become a fish whenever he wished, so sometimes he was represented as leaping into the sea, diving down to great depth, and swimming until he felt the approach of rising land, then he would come to the surface, call out the name of the island and go ashore for a visit with the inhabitants or dive again and pass on to another island. Thus he is represented as passing to Hawaii after his adventures on the islands of Kauai and Oahu.

On Hawaii he entered into the sports of the chiefs, gambling, boxing, surf-riding, rolling the round ulu maika stone and riding the holua (sled). Here he learned about the wonderful princess from the islands of the southern seas who had made her home in the fountains of fire.

Some of the legends say that he returned to Oahu, gathered a company of adherents and then visited the Pele family as a chief of high rank, winning her as his bride and living with her some time, then separating and dividing the island of Hawaii between them, Pele taking the southern part of the island as the scene for her terrific eruptions, and Kamapuaa ruling over the north, watering the land with gentle showers or with melting snow, or sometimes with fierce storms, until for many centuries fertile fields have rewarded the toil of man.

The better legends send Kamapuaa alone to the contest with the fire-goddess, winning her for a time and then entering into a struggle in which both lives were at stake.

It is said that one morning when the tops of the mountains were painted by the sunlight from the sea, and the shadows in the valley were creeping under the leaves of the trees of the forests, that Pele and her sisters went down toward the hills of Puna. These sisters were known as the Hiiakas, defined by Ellis, who gives the first account of them, as "The cloud-holders." Each one had a descriptive title, thus Hiiaka-noho-lani was "The heaven-dwelling cloud-holder," Hiiaka-i-ka-poli-o-Pele was "The cloud-holder in the bosom of Pele." There were at least six Hiiakas, and some legends give many more.

That morning they heard the sound of a drum in the distance. It was the tum-tum-tum of a hula. Filled with curiosity they turned aside to see what strangers had invaded their territory. One of the sisters, looking over the plain to a hill not far away, called out, "What a handsome man!" and asked her sisters to mark the finely formed athletic stranger who was dancing gloriously outlined in the splendor of the morning light.

Pele scornfully looked and said she saw nothing but a great hog-man, whom she would quickly drive from her dominions. Then began the usual war of words with which rival chiefs attacked each other. Pele taunted Kamapuaa, calling him a hog and ascribing to him the characteristics belonging to swine. Kamapuaa became angry and called Pele "the woman with red burning eyes, and an angry heart unfit to be called a chiefess." Then Pele in her wrath stamped on the ground until earthquakes shook the land around Kamapuaa and a boiling stream of lava rolled down from the mountains above. The stranger, throwing around him the finest tapa, stood unmoved until the flood of fire began to roll up the hill on which he stood. Then raising his hands and uttering the strongest incantations he called for heavy rains to fall. Soon the lava became powerless in the presence of the stranger. Then Pele tried her magical powers to see if she could subdue this stranger, but his invocations seemed to be stronger than those falling from her lips, and she gave up the attempt to destroy him. Pele was always a cruel, revengeful goddess, sweeping away those against whom her wrath might be kindled, even if they were close friends of her household.

The sisters finally prevailed upon her to send across to the hill inviting the stranger, who was evidently a high chief, to come and visit them. As the messenger started to bring the young man to the sisters he stepped into the shadows, and the messenger found nothing but a small hog rooting among the ferns. This happened day after day until Pele determined to know this stranger chief who always succeeded in thoroughly hiding himself, no matter how carefully the messengers might search. At last the chant of the hula and the dance of the sisters on the smooth pahoehoe* of a great extinct lava bed led the young man to approach. Pele revealed herself in her rare and tempting beauty, calling with a sweet voice for the stranger to come and rest by her side while her sisters danced. Soon Pele was overcome by the winning strength of this great chief, and she decided to marry him. So they dwelt together in great happiness for a time, sometimes making their home in one part of Puna and sometimes in another. The places where they dwelt are pointed out even at this day by the natives who know the traditions of Puna.

But Kamapuaa had too many of the habits and instincts of a hog to please Pele, besides she was too quickly angry to suit the overbearing Kama-puaa. Pele was never patient even with her sisters, so with Kamapuaa she would burst into fiery rage, while taunts and bitter words were freely hurled back and forth. Then Pele stamped on the ground, the earth shook, cracks opened in the surface and sometimes clouds of smoke and steam arose around Kamapuaa. He

* Pahoehoe, smooth lava. A-a, rough lava.

270

was unterrified and matched his divine powers
against hers. It was demi-god against demi-god-
dess. It was the goddess of fire of Hawaii against
the hog-god of Oahu. Pele's home life was given
up. The bitterness of strife swept over the black
sands of the seashore. When the earth seemed
ready to open its doors and pour out mighty
streams of flowing lava in the defence of Pele,
Kamapuaa called for the waters of the ocean to
rise. Then flood met fire and quenched it. Pele
was driven inland. Her former lover, hastening
after her and striving to overcome her, followed
her upward until at last amid clouds of poiso-
nous gases she went back into her spirit home
in the pit of Kilauea.

Then Kamapuaa as a god of the sea gathered
the waters together in great masses and hurled
them into the firepit. Violent explosions followed the inrush of waters. The sides of the
great crater were torn to pieces by fierce earthquakes. Masses of fire expanded the water into
steam, and Pele gathered the forces of the
underworld to aid in driving back Kamapuaa.
The lavas rose in many lakes and fountains.
Rapidly the surface was cooled and the fountains checked, but just as rapidly were new
openings made and new streams of fire hurled
at the demi-god of Oahu. It was a mighty battle
of the elements. The legends say that the hog-

man, Kamapuaa, poured water into the crater until its fires were driven back to their lowest depths and Pele was almost drowned by the floods. The clouds of the skies had dropped their burden of rain. All the waters of the sea that Kamapuaa could collect had been poured into the crater. Fornander gives a part of the prayer of Kamapuaa against Pele. His appeal was directly to the gods of water for assistance. He cried for

... "The great storm clouds of skie,"
while Pele prayed for
"The bright gods of the under-world,
  The gods thick-clustered for Pele."

It was the duty of the Pele family to stir up volcanic action, create explosions, hurl lava into the air, make earthquakes, blow out clouds of flames and smoke and sulphurous-burdened fumes against all enemies of Pele. Into the conflict against Kamapuaa rushed the gods of Po, the under-world, armed with spears of flashing fire, and hurling sling-stones of lava. The storms of bursting gases and falling lavas were more than Kamapuaa could endure. Gasping for breath and overwhelmed with heat, he found himself driven back. The legends say that Pele and her sisters drank the waters, so that after a time there was no check against the uprising lava. The pit was filled and the streams of fire flowed down upon Kamapuaa. He changed his body into a kind of grass now known as Ku-kae-puaa, and tried to stop the flow of the lava. Apparently the grass represented the bristles covering his body when he changed himself into a hog. Kamapuaa has sometimes been called the Samson of Hawaiian traditions, and it is possible that a Biblical idea has crept into the modern versions of the story. Delilah cut Samson's hair and he became weak. The Hawaiian traditions say that, if Kamapuaa's bristles could be burned off, he would lose his power to cope with Pele's forces of fire. When the grass lay in the pathway of the fire, the lava was turned aside for a time, but Pele, inspired by the beginning of victory, called anew upon the gods of the under-world for strong reinforcements.

Out from the pits of Kilauea came vast masses of lava piling up against the field of grass in its pathway and soon the grass began to burn; then Kamapuaa assumed again the shape of a man, the hair or bristles on his body were singed and the smart of many burns began to cause agony. Down he rushed to the sea, but the lava spread out on either side, cutting off retreat along the beach. Pele followed close behind, striving to overtake him before he could reach the water. The side streams had reached the sea, and the water was rapidly heated into tossing, boiling waves. Pele threw great masses of lava at Kamapuaa, striking and churning the sea into which he leaped midst the swirling heated mass. Kamapuaa gave up the battle, and, thoroughly defeated, changed himself into a fish. To that fish he gave the tough pigskin which he assumed when roaming over the islands as the hog-man. It was thick enough to stand the boiling waves through which he swam out into the deep sea. The Hawaiians say that this fish has always been able to make a noise like the grunting of a small pig. To this fish was given the name "humu-humu-nuku-nuku-a-puaa."

It was said that Kamapuaa fled to foreign lands, where he married a high chiefess and lived with his family many years. At last the longing for his home-land came over him irresistibly and he returned appearing as a humu-humu in his divine place among the Hawaiian fishes, but never again taking to himself the form of a man.

Since this conflict with Kamapuaa, Pele has never feared the powers of the sea. Again and again has she sent her lava streams over the territory surrounding her firepit in the volcano Kilauea, and has swept the seashore, even pouring her lavas into the deep sea, but the ocean has never retaliated by entering into another conflict to destroy Pele and her servants. Kamapuaa was the last who poured the sea into the deep pit. The friends of Lohiau, a prince from the island of Kauai, waged warfare with Pele, tearing to pieces a part of the crater in which she dwelt; but it was a conflict of land forces, and in its entirety is one of the very interesting tales handed down by Hawaiian tradition.

Kamapuaa figured to the last days of Pele-worship in the sacrifices offered to the fire-goddess. The most acceptable sacrifice to Pele was supposed to be puaa (a hog). If a hog could not be secured when an offering was necessary, the priest would take the fish humu-humu-nuku-nuku-a-puaa and throw it into the pit of fire. If the hog and the fish both failed, the priest would offer any of the things into which, it was said in their traditions, Kamapuaa could turn himself.

Note: For more Pele stories see the "Legends of Volcanoes" by the author.

PRONUNCIATION

"A syllable in Hawaiian may consist of a single vowel, or a consonant united with a vowel or at most of a consonant and two vowels, never of more than one consonant. The ac- cent of five-sixths of the words is on the penult, and a few proper names accent the first syllable. In Hawaiian every syllable ends in a vowel and no syllable can have more than three letters, generally not more than two and a large number of syllables consist of single letters— vowels. Hence the vowel sounds greatly predominate over the consonant. The language may therefore appear monot- onous to one unacquainted with its force. In Hawaiian there is a great lack of generic terms, as is the ease with all uncultivated languages. No people have use for generic terms until they begin to reason and the language shows that they were better warriors and poets than philosophers and statesmen. Their language, however, richly abounds in specific names and epithets. The general rule, then, is that the accent falls on the penult; but there are many exceptions and some words which look the same to the eye take on entirely different meanings by different tones, accents, or inflections. The study of these kaaos or legends would demonstrate that the Hawaiians possessed a language not only adapted to their former necessities but capable of being used in introducing the arts of civilized society and especially of pure morals, of law, and the religion of the Bible."

The above quotations are from Lorrin Andrew's Dictionary of the Hawaiian Language, containing some 15,500 Hawaiian words, printed in Honolulu in 1865.

Hawaiian vowels

a	is sounded as in father
e	is sounded as in they
i	is sounded as in marine
o	is souonded as in note
u	is sounded as in rule or as oo in moon
ai	when sounded as a diphthong resembles English *ay*
au	when sounded as a diphthong resembles *ou* as in loud

The consonants are *h, k, l, m, n, p,* and *w.* No distinction is made between *k* and *t* or *l* and *r,* and w sounds like v between the penult and final syllable of a word.

APPENDIX

PARTIAL LIST OF HAWAIIAN TERMS USED

(For Pronunciation, see page 276)